22225/
28.01

R48513

D1556742

KENT·INSTITUTE
OF·ART·&·DESIGN
LIBRARY

Book No.................... Class No./Mark 741.6 mas
This book is to be returned on or before the last date
stamped below.

16. 07

-7 APR 2008

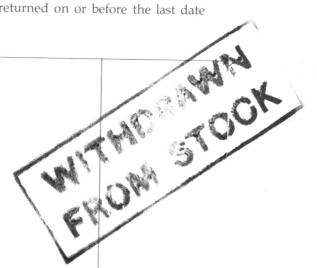

WITHDRAWN FROM STOCK

Publishing house:
BIS Publishers
Nieuwe Spiegelstraat 36
1017 DG Amsterdam
T 0031 20 6205171
F 0031 20 6279251
www.bispublishers.nl
bis@bispublishers.nl

©2003 BIS Publishers, Amsterdam
ISBN 90 6369 048 7

**BIS**PUBLISHERS

# SPACE GRAPHYSM

## HIROMURA MASAAKI

今、デザインはその分類の領域が曖昧なものとなりつつあります。曖昧化が進む中で、デザインの本質が問われているのです。

デザインという職種は、デザインの時代と言われた20世紀の産業構造に裏づけられ、大量に複製し、消費されることによって、細分化され、拡張してきました。グラフィックデザイナーが関わるデザインの領域だけでも、広告・CI・パッケージ・ブック・エディトリアル・サイン・ディスプレイ……と専門性を細分化し、その市場を拡大させてきたわけです。では、この領域が何故曖昧化してきたかというと、理由は次の二つの側面にわかれるのではないでしょうか。

一つは、コンピュータ等の新しい技術の登場による専門的職能への疑いとでもいうべきある種の脅迫観念です。ぞくぞくと開発されるソフトウェアは、長年積み重ねてきた専門技術をいとも簡単に一般供給してしまうし、知識もネットを通して世界中から集め、蓄積することができるからです。この「誰でもデザイナー」的状況が、デザインを安直な方向へと向かわせていることも現実です。

もう一つは、社会の多様化・複雑化に伴い、デザインが解決すべきテーマが複雑に重層化していることです。従来のカテゴリーでは解決できない難題がデザイナーにつきつけられています。

私はこのような現状を決して悲観せず、むしろ、デザインの本質を再構築するチャンスだと考えています。

近年生まれた「情報デザイン」という言葉は、ウェブデザインや先端技術系の領域を示すだけでなく、デザインの本質を表した言葉として捉えています。

デザインは、ある目的を持って情報を相手に伝える、メッセージを送るという仕事です。つまり、デザインとは広義には情報であり、その情報を整理・再構築・伝達することがデザインと言えます。

複雑で多様な情報は、わかりやすく、魅力的に再構築することで新たな価値を生み出します。また、技術は時代と共に進化し淘汰されていくのが宿命です。人と人・人と社会・人と科学・人と芸術といった関係性の中で、良質な「対話」を生み出す知恵がデザインの役割だと考えています。

この本では、サインシステムや空間演出など、グラフィックデザインを基軸に、異領域とコラボレイトした仕事を集めています。

デザインの本質を認識し、良質な対話を重ねていった時の、互いに融合と分裂を経て進化していく過程が紹介できればと思います。

Designs are becoming increasingly interdisciplinary. While the borders between different design genres are blurred, it is questioned what design is.

Supported by the industrial structure in the 20th century which was called "an age of design," designs were massively duplicated and consumed. During this time, design has been expanded greatly while branching out into many small segments. In the design field that graphic designers are related, specialization progressed into advertisements, Corporate Identity (Image), packages, books, editorial designs, signs, displays and so on, and the entire market for designers has been widened. Why have the borders become blurred? Two aspects for this can be considered.

One is a kind of skepticism and a feeling of our profession being threatened as a result of the advent of computers and other advanced technologies. Software programs developed one after another popularized the professional techniques that have been accumulated among experts for a long time. Information can be collected through the Internet from all over the world. This "everyone can be a designer" situation is promoting easy-going tendencies in the world of design.

Another aspect is that along with the diversification and complication of the society, subjects that designers deal with are complicatedly layered. Now, challenging problems are placed under designers' nose, which cannot be solved within traditional design genres. I do not feel pessimistic about this situation, rather, I find it a good chance to consider the essential function of designers.

I understand the new design genre "Information Design" that emerged in recent years not only as web design and designing for other advanced technologies but also as the term to imply the essence of design. Designing is a kind of work to convey information or messages to others with a specific purpose. In a broad sense, design itself is information, and the process of sorting, compiling and actually conveying it to the public. Value can be added to complicated information when it is reconstructed in a more easy-to-understand, attractive way.

Technologies are invented and only selected ones remain to be used. The role of designers is to incite a dialogue between persons, between persons and society, persons and science, and persons and art.

In this book, sign systems, space creations and other collaboration works of graphic designers with those from different genres are presented.

I hope we can show the process of fusion and split during our collaborative work through discussion on the essence of design.

741.6
mas

# SYSTEM

# GRAPHYSM

# PRESENTAT

# VISUAL IDE

# SYSTEM

海外の都市ではじめて地下鉄に乗ろうと思い、システムがわからず途方にくれたことがあります。

チケットの買い方やホームまでのアクセス、電車の乗り降りと、まったく初めて体験するシステムは、すぐ馴染むものとなかなか慣れないものがあるのが現実です。

多くの人が利用する施設では、情報をわかりやすく伝える為に、体系的なシステムが必要です。サインデザインの場合、施設全体が共通のシステムでコントロールされている状況を、人々が早い段階で認識できると、その後の行動をスムーズに誘導することが可能となります。なるべくシンプルな考え方のシステムが結果的にわかりやすいサインですが、施設や環境での目的や内容は様々で、一概にわかりやすいという視点だけでシステムを考えることは良い環境づくりにつながりません。施設独特の目的をふまえ、人々の意識にいかに働きかけていくか、ということがシステム構築する際に欠かすことのできないものだからです。

システムというと難しいイメージがありますが、たとえば「青」というテーマでシステムを組むとしましょう。「青」の色はシステムのベースになります。それを中心に他の情報要素（文字、ピクト、マップ等）と組み合わせることでシステムの骨格を創ります。

この時、常に「青と情報」は、ユーザーと目的を結ぶサインコネクターなのです。基本情報の窓口として機能し、青＝情報として人々の意識に刷り込まれていくことになります。

システムは複雑な情報を解読する方程式ですが、人々の意識にポジティブに働きかけていくためには、魅力的なデザインのクオリティが必要です。

I tried to take a subway in a foreign country, and I was at a loss how to buy a ticket, how to go to the platform, which direction to take and so on. Some systems are easy to get used to, while others are not.

A well-organized sign system is required for any facility that many people use. When the visitors recognize at an early stage that the whole facility is controlled by a common sign system, they can move freely guided by the signs. A simple sign system is easier for the visitors. However, as every facility and space has different purposes and characteristics, it may not be advisable to plan a system only for the sake of easiness. An understanding about the purpose of a facility, and thinking about the ways to act upon the users of the facility are important elements in building a sign system.

Suppose we create a system with "blue" as the main motif. The base color is blue, and other information elements (letters, pictograms, maps) are combined to build the framework of the system.

Here, "blue and information elements" are connectors for the users to reach their destinations. The users realize that blue gives them useful information.

A system is a formula to decipher complicated information, and to act upon people's minds positively, design must be attractive.

岩出山町立岩出山中学校

サインディレクション：廣村正彰
デザイン：廣村正彰、相澤信彦
建築設計：山本理顕
家具設計：榎本文夫、黒川勉
コーディネーション：山崎あかね
施工：松村組
クライアント：岩出山町

Iwadeyama Junior High School

sign direction : Hiromura Masaaki
design : Hiromura Masaaki,
Aizawa Nobuhiko
architect : Yamamoto Riken
furniture design : Enomoto Fumio,
Kurokawa Tsutomu
coordination : Yamazaki Akane
construction : Matsumura-gumi
client : Iwadeyama Town

埼玉県立大学

アートディレクション：廣村正彰
デザイン：廣村正彰、相澤信彦
建築設計：山本理顕
家具設計：近藤康夫、黒川勉、山中俊治
アートワーク：舟橋全二（サインコラボレーション）
アートコーディネーション：コトブキ
タウンアート事業部
コーディネーション：山崎あかね
施工：岡村製作所、コトブキ
クライアント：埼玉県立大学

Saitama Prefectural University

art direction : Hiromura Masaaki
design : Hiromura Masaaki,
Aizawa Nobuhiko
architect : Yamamoto Riken
furniture design : Kondoh Yasuo,
Kurokawa Tsutomu, Yamanaka Toshiharu
art work : Funabashi Zenji
(sign collaboration)
art coordination : Kotobuki Town Art
coordination : Yamazaki Akane
construction : Okamura, Kotobuki
client : Saitama Prefectural University

公立はこだて未来大学

アートディレクション：廣村正彰
デザイン：廣村正彰、前田豊
建築設計：山本理顕
家具設計：近藤康夫、山中俊治、森田敏昭
コーディネーション：山崎あかね
クライアント：公立はこだて未来大学

Future University-Hakodate

art direction : Hiromura Masaaki
design : Hiromura Masaaki,
Maeda Yutaka
architect : Yamamoto Riken
furniture design : Kondoh Yasuo,
Yamanaka Toshiharu, Morita Toshiaki
coordination : Yamazaki Akane
client : Future University-Hakodate

008    IWADEYAMA JUNIOR HIGH SCHOOL

Toilet

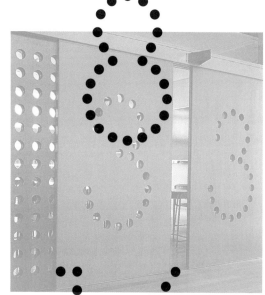

Toile

男子卓球部

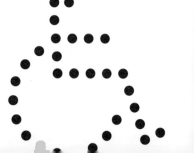

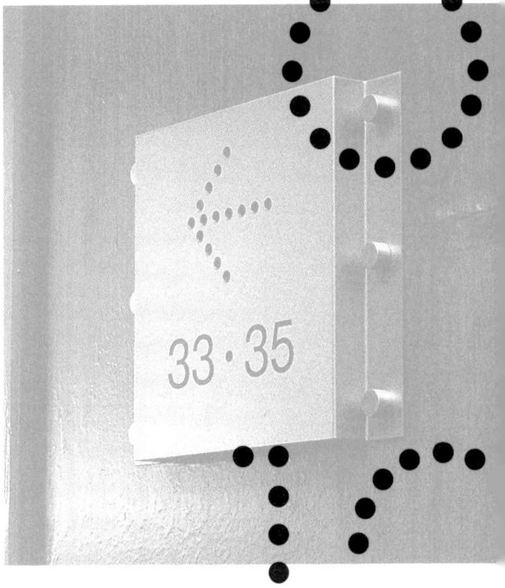


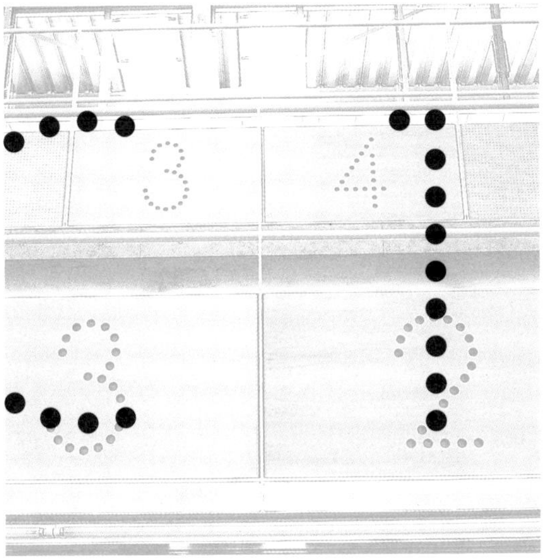




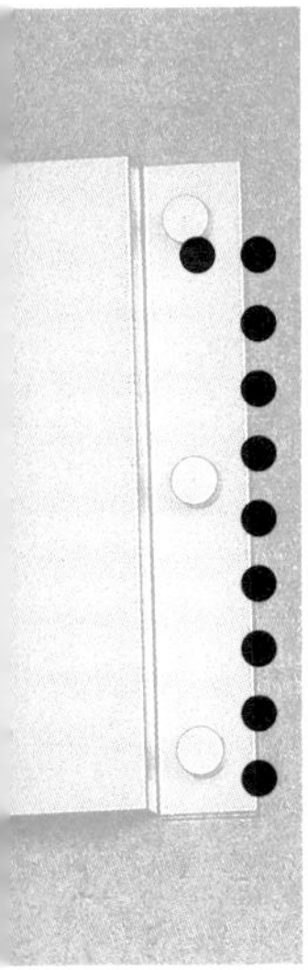

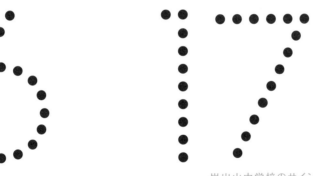

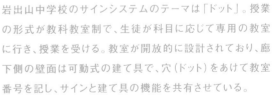

岩出山中学校のサインシステムのテーマは「ドット」。授業の形式が教科教室制で、生徒が科目に応じて専用の教室に行き、授業を受ける。教室が開放的に設計されており、廊下側の壁面は可動式の建て具で、穴（ドット）をあけて教室番号を記し、サインと建て具の機能を共有させている。

The motif for the Iwadeyama Junior High School Sign System was "dot." The classrooms are arranged according to subjects, and students travel from one room to another according to their time schedule. The school takes an open-classroom style. The partition walls on the corridor side are movable. Room numbers are punched like dots on the walls.

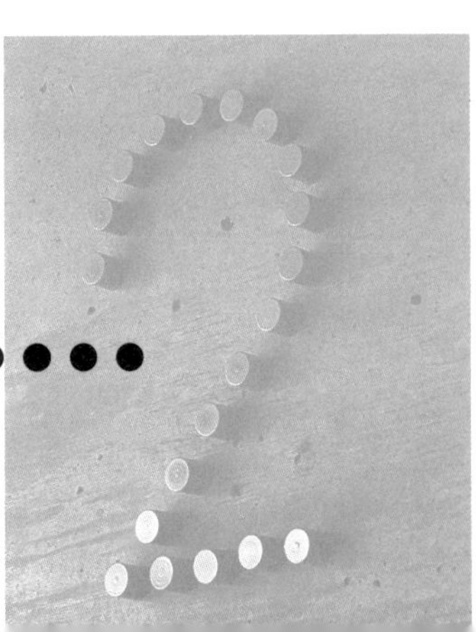

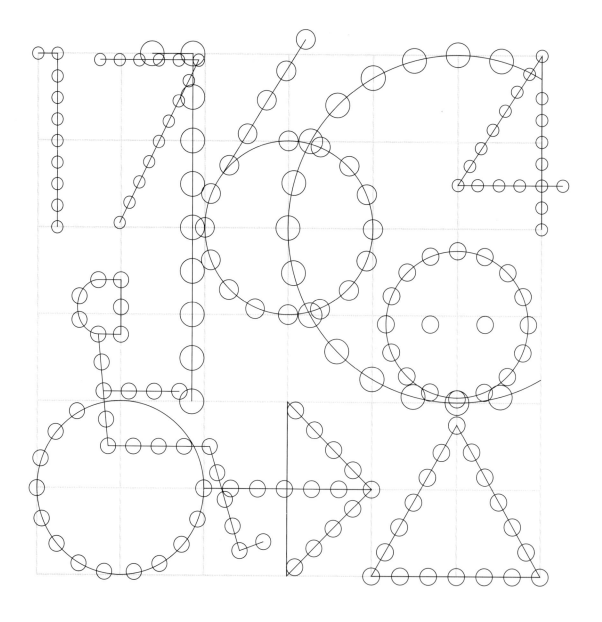

教室の建て具に穴をあけ、内部と外部の境界意識をあいまいにすることで、サインの機能だけではなく、学校という教育空間の意識を変えることになった。建て具のプランがきっかけになり、全体をドットのサインでシステムを構築するために、数字やピクトグラムをオリジナルで開発した。

By blurring the border between the outside and inside of the classroom by punching holes on the walls, people's consciousness about classrooms changed. Numbers and pictograms to be used for dotted signs were developed specifically for this sign system.

ドットのサインシステムは、校門から始まり、室名、誘導案内、階数表示、ロッカー番号等それぞれ目的や内容に合わせて表現や素材を変えている。結果的に生徒達はそれまでの学校に比べ、自由度が高く開放的な環境にすぐ適応し、自分達で新たな空間の使い方を発見している。

The dot sign system begins with the gate, and used for rooms, guideposts, floors, and lockers all made with different materials and expressions. Students immediately adapted to this open-style environment with greater freedom and began to make creative use of the space.

埼玉県立大学は、広大な敷地に一辺が
200mの大学棟と短大棟が両サイドに建っ
ている。中庭は2階がテラスで、1階は実験室
や演習室、図書館などが複雑に入り組む共通
施設棟。それは少し迷路のようになっていて、
一度入ると方向感覚もあやしくなる。そこで
アート計画の一貫として、人型の壁面オブジェ
をつくり、サインの機能をもたせ、迷路のどの
地点に立ってもサインが見えるように設置した。

In the huge Saitama Prefectural University campus, 200 meter-long university and junior college buildings are built facing each other. In the yard between the two are facilities used by both students. The roofs are used as terraces. On the ground floor, laboratories, a library, seminar rooms and others are arranged complicatedly. It is like a maze, and once you enter, you may lose the sense of direction. Therefore, we created figure objects and attached them at places that would be visible from any point in the maze.

人型のアートと一体化したサインマップは、
パースペクティブに描かれており、取り付け
られた方向により変化する。また厚い鉄板に
黒く塗装された人型アートは、手を伸ばしたり、
ゆったり歩いたり、人の動作を大胆なシルエ
ット表現でシンボライズしている。サインの
機能をアートと合体させることにより、アート
の存在感が浮き彫りにされ、キャンパスの中
では重要な役割を果たしている。

The maps with figure art works are drawn in perspective representation. They are different depending on the place of installation. The silhouette figures stretching a hand, walking slowly, and so on are made with black iron sheets. The functions of sign and art are integrated through this method.

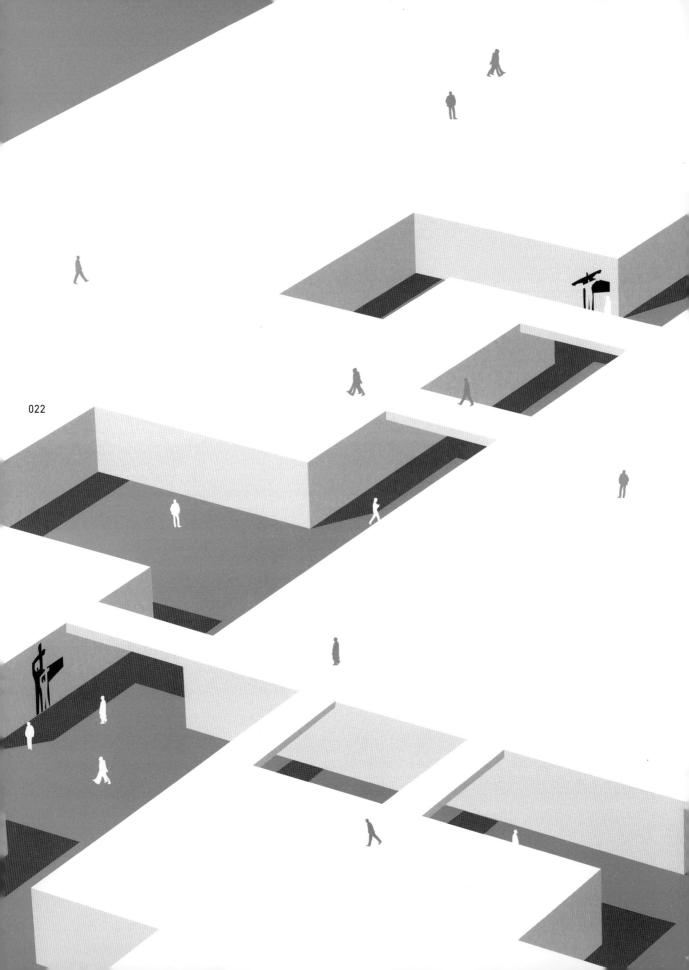

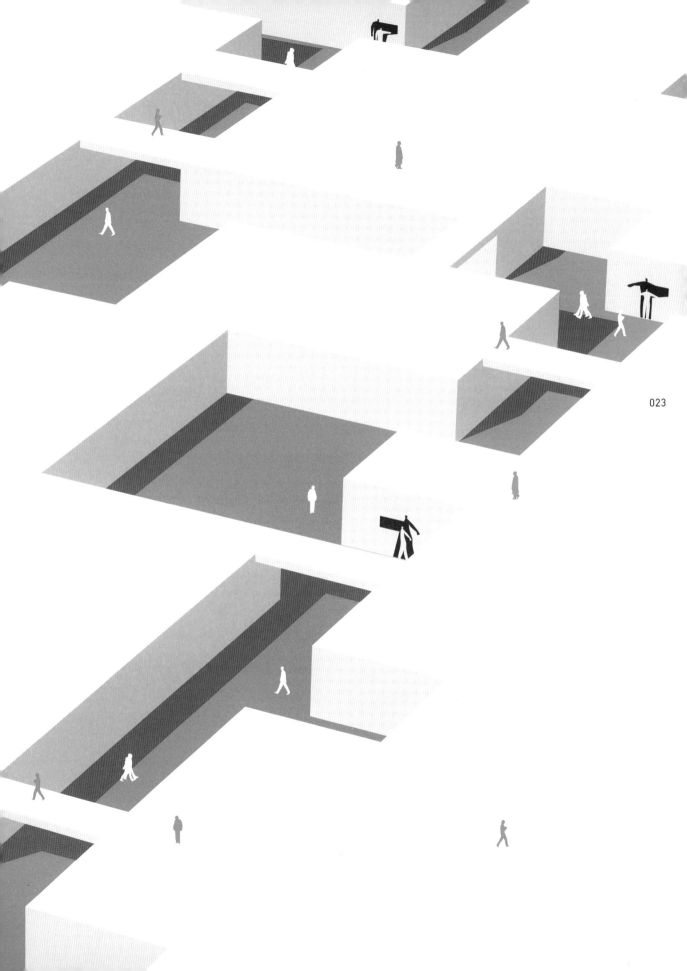

大学棟と短大棟は一辺が200mの長さで、テラスを間にしてそれぞれ向き合っている。建物はPC（プレキャストコンクリート）が縦方向に等間隔に組まれており、教室や講義室はテラスから見ると、目的の部屋を瞬間に判別するには難しい。PCとPCの間に天井から大きな室番号を吊るし、遠方からでも視認できるように設置した。

Two 200-meter long school buildings are facing each other with a terrace in between. They are constructed with pre-cast concrete structures aligned with an equal interval. From the terrace, it is difficult to identify a specific room at sight. In order to improve visibility, a large number is hung from the ceiling.

45

215

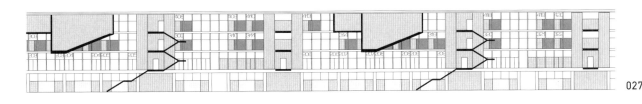

317

番号表記は階数と2桁の部屋数を並べて、全て3桁に統一した。三つの組み合わされた数字は、一つずつ天井に取り付けることが、技術と強度の関係で不可能になり、三つそれぞれお互いに繋がっている事が条件になった。そこで新しく数字を開発し、上下左右のバランスを取るために繋げた三つの数字の長さになるべく差が出ないようにした。

A room number is composed of three digits, the first one indicating the floor and the last two indicating a room number. It was found technically impossible to hang three numbers separately, and a three-digit number had to be hung as a unit. Therefore, new 3-digit numbers were made endeavoring to make their size as equal as possible.

333

133

数字を強調したサインは、教室から始まり、図書館の閲覧室や、書架にも反映させた。ステンレス鏡面で作られた書架はミラーの効果により、収蔵している書籍を写し出し、書架自体のボリュームを消している。白い数字のサインが写り込んだ書籍に浮かび、不思議な空間を作り出している。

The number signs are employed also for the bookshelves and reading rooms in the library. Stainless steel bookshelves mirror books in other shelves, and make the bookshelves look as if they have no volume.  White number signs appear to float above the books.  These, altogether, create a strange space.

サインで使われるマップは、全てパースになっており、自分の現在位置と方向、目的との距離感をインプットできるようなグラフィックにした。マップが不要な誘導の為のサインも、方向性が分かるようにパースの表現を使い、サイン全体のシステムがスムーズに理解できるように図の形式を統一している。

All the maps were drawn with perspective presentation. With this, the visitors can easily identify where they are, and the direction and distance to their destinations. For guidepost signs, the same method was utilized to indicate the directions. The style of graphics is uniformed in this way to help the visitors obtain an idea of the entire sign system.

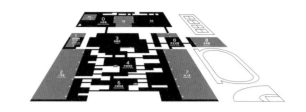

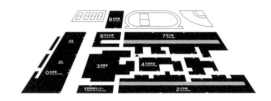

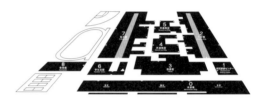

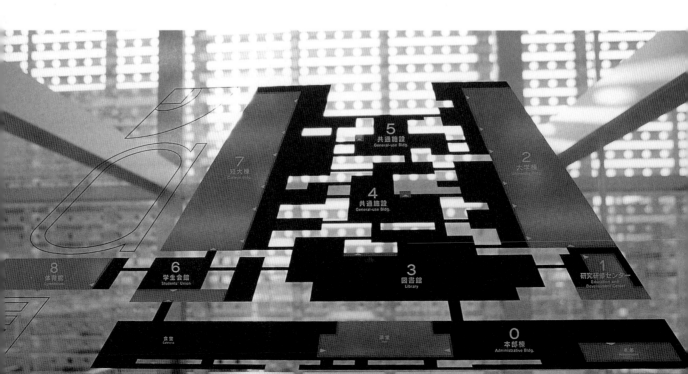

# 2 大学棟
## University Bldg.

346 大講義室 Large Lecture Room

332 大講義室 Large Lecture Room

# 4 共通施設
## General-use Bldg.

| | | | | |
|---|---|---|---|---|
| 小演習室<br>Small Lecture Room | **120** | **121** | 中演習室<br>Lecture Room |
| 小演習室<br>Small Lecture Room | **119** | **122** | 中演習室<br>Lecture Room |
| 小演習室<br>Small Lecture Room | **118** | **123** | 中演習室<br>Lecture Room |
| 小演習室<br>Small Lecture Room | **117** | **124** | 中演習室<br>Lecture Room |
| 小演習室<br>Small Lecture Room | **116** | **125** | 中演習室<br>Lecture Room |
| 小演習室<br>Small Lecture Room | **115** | **126** | 中演習室<br>Lecture Room |

| 建築はコラボレートのフィールドだ |
| 山本理顕 × 廣村正彰 |

## コラボレーションは変化への導線

廣村:「岩出山町立岩出山中学校」の初めのプランでは、扉に大きなドット（穴）がボンボンと開いていたんですよ。ならばサインもドットでやってみたいと思って。「サインで穴を使っていいですか」と山本さんに尋ねたところから始まりましたね。

山本:廣村さんと話しているうちに、全部、穴を開けて数字を表記してしまおうということになった。そのうち、どこまでが廣村さんで、どこまでが僕なのか、やっているうちにわからなくなってしまうんです。表面の扱いも装飾的だったものが即物的になっていったり、どんどんこちらの頭が変わっていくのがわかる。デザイナーに触発されて自分がこんな風に変化して、建築まで変わっていってしまうということを体験して、すごく面白かった。ほんの小さなきっかけであっても、これほどまでに変われるということが僕にはすごく新鮮で、まさにコラボレーションの醍醐味に出会ったと思いましたね。

廣村:僕にもたくさんの発見がありました。山本さんが異なる視点からあらゆる方向でディスカッションをしてくれたことが、サインを考えていく時に大きな手掛かりを与えてくれました。こういうのはどうだとか、駄目だとか、面白いとか。雑談のなかからも多くのヒントをもらいました。未知の部分があるなかで手掛かりを掴んでいかなければならないサインデザインでは、「発見する」という作業はとても重要なんです。その何かが見つかった時はすごく面白いことができる。

山本:その発見も一人で発見するのと、コラボレーション作業のなかで発見するのとでは全く違うと思う。

廣村:本来のコラボレーションという意味が分かったような気がしました。だんだんサインデザインの範囲を超えていってしまう。

山本:それが建築にまで変化を与えていくことになった。「穴を開けて数字を表記する」という方法を全てに取り入れてしまいましたからね。

## サインデザインと建築プランの相乗効果

山本:確かに、「岩出山中学校」は、その後の僕の作品にずいぶん影響を与えました。それまでジョイントなどのディテールに何かしら装飾的な要素を持ち込んでいたのが、もっと即物的になった。そのきっかけは、廣村さんたちとコラボレーションしたことで得た外部からの刺激が大きかった。「CODAN Shinonome 1街区」などは、まさにカラーが建築の表現そのものになっているし、廣村さんと仕事をしていると、いつも

## Buildings are fields for collaboration
## Yamamoto Riken × Hiromura Masaaki

Collaboration triggers changes.

Hiromura: The initial plan for Iwadeyama Junior High School showed the door with large holes like dots. And I thought that I would apply dots also for signs, and asked you if I could use dotted holes for signs. That was the beginning of our collaboration.

Yamamoto: During our discussion, we agreed to show numerals all with holes. Once we began doing the work, I could hardly separate the sphere of responsibility between yours and mine. My surface treatment was decorative at the beginning, but it gradually became simpler. It was an interesting experience that I realized that my thinking was influenced by a designer and my architectural design changed consequently. It was a fresh discovery to see that I can change my thinking this much. I felt that I was enjoying the thrill of collaboration.

Hiromura: I also had many discoveries. We approached our discussions from different angles and I found hints in designing signs. Even during our free talks, as you said "this is good, that is no good," I obtained many hints. In designing signs, we must find hints for design from information, although not all information is clearly known yet. So, to discover some hint is very important, and when I find some hint, I can create something very interesting.

Yamamoto: That discovery may be different from what you might discover alone.

Hiromura: I realized the meaning of collaboration in its true sense. I gradually crossed the border of sign design.

Yamamoto: And it exerted influence on architecture, because we applied the design concept of "cut holes to express figures" to the entire schoolhouse.

Synergetic Effects of Sign Design and Architectural Plan

Yamamoto: The Iwadeyamal Junior High School gave impact on my latter works. Until then, I introduced decorative elements to joints and other details, but after this school, I changed my style. The stimuli I had through working with you and others were great. In the "Codan Shinonome District 1,"

僕は建築で下地をつくっているようなものですよ。

**廣村：**基本的には山本さんのアイデアですよ。いきなりレインボーカラーを建築そのものに展開したのは山本さんですから。

山本：玄関ホール部分のポストに施されたストライプカラーがきれいですごく面白かったから、いっそ建物全部の各階を同じようにダーッとストライプで埋めてしまおうと思ったんです。

**廣村：**「甃甌の絵のように」という発想も山本さんならではの面白さですよね。それにしても、空間と関わるということはこんなに面白いのだから、グラフィックデザイナーの人ももっと建築に関わったデザインをすればいいのにと思う。

山本：実際問題として「建築にかかわるサインデザイナー」というのは相当柔軟じゃないと難しいと思います。

**廣村：**カテゴリーとしては、まだ成立しきれていませんからちょっと辛いでしょうね。現実として、サインは建築やインテリアや家具の「オマケ」のようなものとして認識されていることが多い。しかし、本当はとても重要な役割を担うはずのカテゴリーなのではないでしょうか。建築物というのは、単体で完結しているわけではなく、家具やサインから、果ては広告活動や広報活動まで、いろいろな要素や動きがあって、一つのイメージとして成り立つのではないかと思うのですが。


知るチャンスを創出するグラフィック


山本：たとえば「Shinonome」の広告・広報のアートディレクションを担当している大貫卓也さんは、今回のプロジェクトで制作した「CODAN」というロゴを、今後開発される都市基盤整備公団の全ての建物に展開することを前提にグラフィックを考えたいと言いました。東雲（しののめ）という一地区のプロジェクトに限定せずに、もっと公団住宅全体を見据えながら、公団の根本的なところで考えているんですよね。廣村さんもそういうところがあるんです。建築自体にまで介入して、建築そのものをも変えてしまうような位置でデザインを考えている。

**廣村：**大貫さんは、広告でどのように効果を上げるかということを、ものすごくシビアに考えている人ですからね。そうなるとどんどんアイデアがシンプルな形になっていってしまうというのはありますね。とにかく、小手先の表現だけでは何も解決しません。根本的な骨格の部分をつくることによって、面白いことに全体がふっと浮き上がってくるんです。たとえば建築のプロジェクトというのは、一般の人たちにしてみれば、実際に何が行われているのか、山本さんたち建築家がどういう動きをしているのかを知るチャンスは、竣工するまでほとんどありません。その唯一の知るチャンスが、新聞広告や雑誌の記事なのです。ロゴや広告などがメディアに載って何十万の目に触れ、そこで初めて存在が露わになってくる。そこにおそらくグラフィックの役割が出てくると思う。

colors are the main elements in the architectural design. When I work with you, I feel like I am preparing the ground for your work.

Hiromura: No, no, it was your idea basically. It was you yourself that introduced rainbow colors into the building.

Yamamoto: The colored stripes used for the mailboxes in the entrance hall were so beautiful and enchanting, so I thought, "Why not? I will give a color to each floor, so that the whole building can be painted in color stripes."

Hiromura: Your idea "like paintings by Ai Oh" is a specific conception no other person would have. It is interesting to design for spaces, I wish many other graphic designers would be involved in spaces.

Yamamoto: It may be difficult for sign designers to be involved in architecture unless they have very flexible thinking.

Hiromura: As it is not established as one design category, we may be faced with many difficulties. Sign design is considered as "supplementary" to architecture and interior architecture. In fact, it is an essential part of a building, because one construction project also involves furniture, signs, and even advertisement and publicity. It is an aggregation of all genres of design.

Graphics as a channel of information to the public

Yamamoto: Onuki Takuya is involved in the Shinonome Project as an art director for its publicity and advertisement. He is thinking to use the logo of "Codan" that he developed for this project for all future buildings built by the Urban Development Corporation (Codan). Based on this idea, he wants to consider graphics for the project. He does not limit his idea to this project alone, but considers that the housing projects by the Corporation. You have something like that. You are thinking about your design at a position from where you intervene with an architectural design and change it.

Hiromura: Onuki is particularly concerned about how effective an advertisement is. And ideas for graphics tend to be expressed in simple forms. When the fundamental framework is solidly made, the entire project comes to surface. For example, people do not have a chance to know what is actually going on in a construction site, or what architects are doing for the project until the construction is completed. The only channel by which the public can learn abut it is a newspaper advertisement or a magazine article. When the logo and advertisement appears in the media and is exposed to millions of people, people come to know about the project. And here is the role that graphic design plays.

山本：現在取り組んでいる2007年開館の「横須賀市立美術館（仮称）」にしてもそうなんですが、ロゴを先につくるほうがいいと言ったのは、そこなんです。クライアントにとっても、メディアを通して知る一般の人たちにとっても、ロゴがあれば建物が実在していなくても具体的な対象物として実感できるようになりますからね。

廣村：ビジュアルで先にイメージをつくると、意識が盛り上がるということですよね。

山本：そうなんです。ロゴタイプが美術館を象徴するものとなって美術館の活動が始まっていく。

## ビジュアルは社会へのプレゼンテーター

廣村：そう考えてみると、ビジュアルというのはものすごく力がある。目に見える形が存在するということは、それだけでリアリティを帯びていくものだと思います。建築が完成するより早く、事前にイメージを形にすることで、意識を高めたり、価値観を共有したり、建築そのものの持つイメージを代行させてわかりやすく伝えていくことができる。グラフィックの側から言うと、環境や空間が出来上がる前段階のヴィジュアルプレゼンテーションをするということは、これからのグラフィックデザインの大きな役割かもしれないし、そこにもグラフィックデザインの新しい活路があるような気がします。

山本：社会のなかでどう役に立っていくか、ということでしょうか。建築もそう言える部分があるかもしれません。建築自体が何に役立っているかということを考えていかないと、なかなか役に立つ建築にならなくなってきている気がしている。社会と具体的にどんな関わり方ができるかを考えていかなければならないと思う。

廣村：低成長時代だという社会的背景もあるとは思いますが、グラフィック自体が今、どんどんシンプルナイズしているところがあるんですね。ある種の原点回帰のようなものかもしれません。余計なものを外していきながら、本質を捉えようとするような、そういう方向が今、グラフィックにも建築にもあるのかもしれません。

山本：建築にもそういうところがあるかもしれない。でも、シンプルがいいからと言って、形だけシンプルにしても何にもならない。形ではなく意識がどうあるのかを考えなければいけないところに来ているのだと思います。

廣村：デザイン自体が形態論とかアイデア論だけではなくなってきている。それに潜む本質をどう捉えるかということになりつつあるのではないでしょうか。表層の形も大事だけれど、根本を考えていくことがこれからは大事だと思います。

## カテゴリーを超えたコラボレートを

廣村：現実として、グラフィックデザインというカテゴリーは、その範囲がかなり曖昧になってきていると思います。たとえば1枚のポスター自身が持つ波及力は以前程大き

Yamamoto: I am now working for an Art Museum in Yokosuka city to be opened in 2007. I proposed that the logo should be designed first. This is because the client and the public who know about it through the media will have a concrete image of the museum even before it is actually built.

Hiromura: If we create an image by visual media, people's awareness is enhanced. Is that right?

Yamamoto: That's right. The logotype becomes a symbol of the museum and activities to construct the museum get started.

Visuals are Means of Presentation to the Market

Hiromura: Visuals have strong influence. Visible forms may give one a feeling of reality about something that is not completed. Making the image of a facility before its construction helps propagate the image of the facility, enhance the public awareness and promote their sharing of values. This may be the most important role for graphic designers, to make a visual presentation before a facility, be it a public space or an environment, is constructed. It may give us a new area of work.

Yamamoto: It may be the role that graphic designers play for society. The same thing may be said of architects. We must consider if a building that we are going to design will play a useful role in society. We must consider how a building can relate with society.

Hiromura: Graphics now are increasingly simplified, which may be an effect of low economic growth in recent years, doing away with decorative elements and expressing the essence straight away. This tendency may be seen both in graphics and architecture.

Yamamoto: There may be such a tendency in architecture. However, simplicity only in outlook does not mean anything. More important is the consciousness of the architect about the relation with society.

Hiromura: Designs can no longer be discussed from the theories of form and concept. We must express how we understand the essence of the subject matter. The surface is important for a design but the fundamental essence will become more important.

Collaboration across design categories

Hiromura: In fact, the border of graphic design is becoming less clear. A poster no longer has the influence that one used to have before. It is not the matter of design quality, but a poster has become only part of the whole publicity strategy using the mass media. Directions are often given by

いものではありません。それはデザイン表現の良し悪しより、メディア戦略として、媒体の1コマでしかなくなってきているからです。そうなると、デザインはメディア主導で決まるようになり、メディアの威力にデザインが追従せざるを得なくなる。そうなりつつある今、グラフィックの本来の活路、本来の役割はどこにあるのか。その一つの解答が空間との関わりのなかにあるような気がします。グラフィックデザインは他のデザイン分野より自己完結しやすいんです。良く言えば、純粋なので、もっと他分野の人と交わることで可能性がどんどん広がります。

山本：もともと建築はコラボレーションによって成立しているものです。古くはフレスコ画家や彫刻家たちと、現代では設備事務所や構造事務所と組みながら建築はつくられてきました。たとえば、柱を細くしたい場合には、最終的には構造事務所の人のデザイン能力が非常に重要になります。空調の位置を工夫したいという話になれば設備事務所の人がアイデアを出す。僕ら建築家の役割というのは「こういう建築にしたい」という方向性を示すことなのです。

廣村：建築家が作成するプランというのは、僕らグラフィックと同様に仮想空間で、現実化はコラボレーションによって行われるということになる。そう考えると山本さんが僕らグラフィックの人間と組むのはあながち不思議なことではない。

山本：建築というのは、みんなで話し合うためのフィールドをつくること。現実の建築こそがフィールドであり、一緒につくっているという意識を共有できるということこそ、建築の面白さです。これがわかってきたのも、廣村さんをはじめ、建築というカテゴリーを超えたコラボレーションをしてきたからこそだと思います。小綺麗にまとめることを志向する人たちではなく、できるだけ大きく描こうとする人たちと出会えたから、刺激的な発見ができる。

廣村：根本を考えていけるコラボレーションは、建築の側ばかりでなくグラフィックにとっても、これから大事なことだと思いますね。

038

山本理顕　建築家
1945年神奈川県生まれ。日本大学理工学部建築学科卒業。東京芸術大学大学院美術研究科建築専攻修了。山本理顕設計工場主宰。主な受賞に88年・02年日本建築学会賞、97年・00年・01年・02年BCS賞、98年毎日芸術賞、99年グッドデザイン賞金賞、01年日本芸術院賞等。主な作品に「熊本県営保田窪第一団地」、「岩出山町立岩出山中学校」、「埼玉県立大学」、「公立はこだて未来大学」、「広島市西消防署」他。著書に『細胞都市』（INAX刊）、『住居論』（住まいの図書館出版局刊）等がある。

media people and we work as their subordinate. When looking for an area in which we can find our own active role, I find graphics for spaces is an answer. Graphic designs are self-complete in nature comparing with other design categories, so graphic designers have not interacted with designers of other genres. But I think we can expand the area of our activities by having contact with people of other fields.

Yamamoto: Architecture is a collaboration of many designers, from the beginning. In the ancient times, architects worked with fresco painters or sculptors, and now with utility equipment offices or structural design offices. If I want to make pillars thinner, we need the design competence of a structural design office. If I want to install an air conditioner at a specific place, then I look to a utility equipment office for advice. The main responsibility of us architects is to show the direction that "I would like to make this building in this way."

Hiromura: The plan that an architect makes is a virtual space, which is the same to graphic works, and the work of giving it concrete shape is a process of collaboration. Considering this, it is not strange that you work in partnership with us in graphic design.

Yamamoto: Architecture is to provide a common field for discussion. An architectural project is a field for collaboration through which all involved can share a feeling of creating something together. Here is the excitement of architecture. I came to realize this after working with you and other designers outside architecture design. Because I have encountered with people who are oriented to design things as magnificent as possible instead of neat designs, I was stimulated to have new discoveries.

Hiromura: It will become more important also for graphic designers to collaborate with architects as it gives us opportunities to consider the fundamentals for graphic design.

Yamamoto Riken, Architect

Born in Kanagawa in 1945. Graduated from Architecture Department, College of Science and Technology, Nihon University. Finished Architecture and Planning course, Fine Arts, Post-graduate School of Tokyo National University of Fine Arts and Music. President of Yamamoto Riken Architecture Workshop. Received the Award of the Architectural Institute of Japan in 1988 and 2002, BCS Award in 1997, 2000, 2001 and 2002, Mainichi Art Award in 1998, Gold Medal of Good Design Award in 1999, Japan Art Academy Award in 2001. Major works include the "Kumanoto Prefectural Hodakubo Housing Complex," "Iwadeyama Junior High School," "Saitama Prefectural University," "Future University-Hakodate," "Hiroshima West Fire Station," and so on. Author of *Cell City* (INAX), and *Theory of Dwelling* (Library of Residences Press).

FUTURE UNIVERSITY-HAKODATE

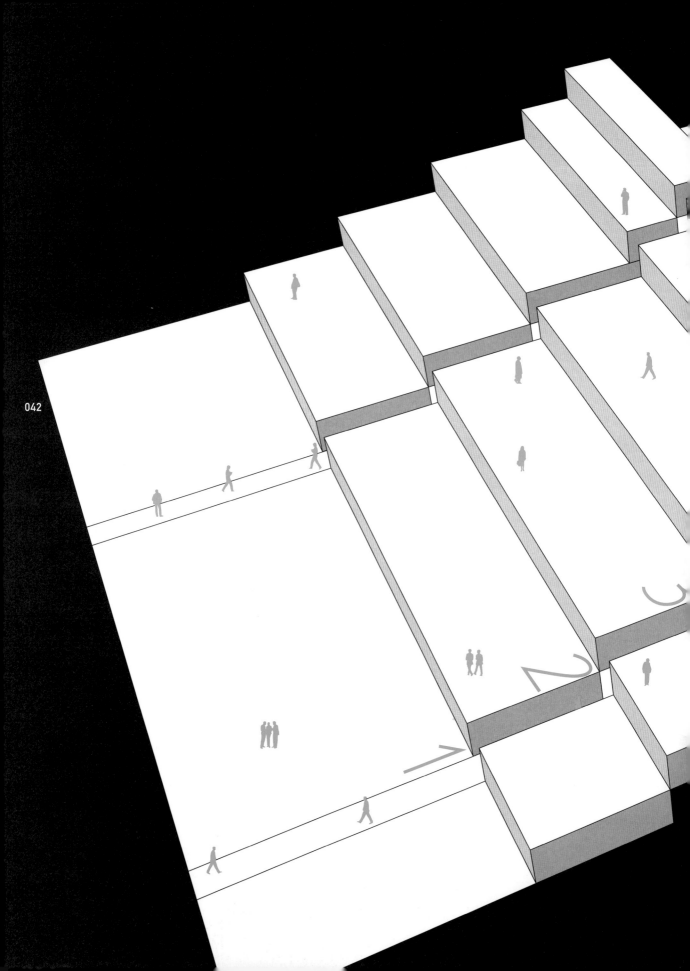

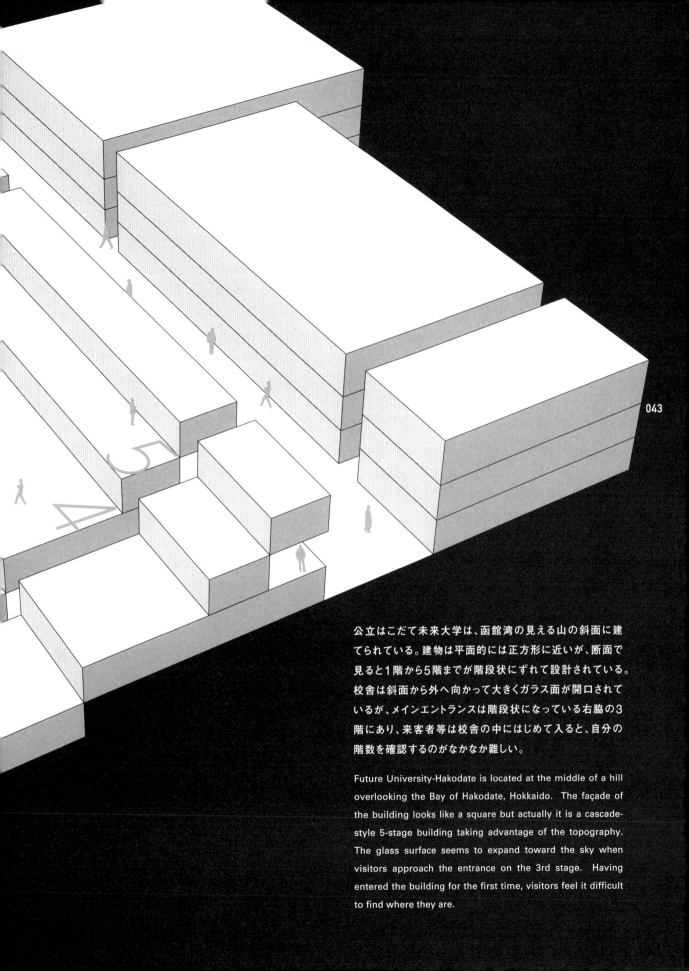

公立はこだて未来大学は、函館湾の見える山の斜面に建てられている。建物は平面的には正方形に近いが、断面で見ると1階から5階までが階段状にずれて設計されている。校舎は斜面から外へ向かって大きくガラス面が開口されているが、メインエントランスは階段状になっている右脇の3階にあり、来客者等は校舎の中にはじめて入ると、自分の階数を確認するのがなかなか難しい。

Future University-Hakodate is located at the middle of a hill overlooking the Bay of Hakodate, Hokkaido. The façade of the building looks like a square but actually it is a cascade-style 5-stage building taking advantage of the topography. The glass surface seems to expand toward the sky when visitors approach the entrance on the 3rd stage. Having entered the building for the first time, visitors feel it difficult to find where they are.

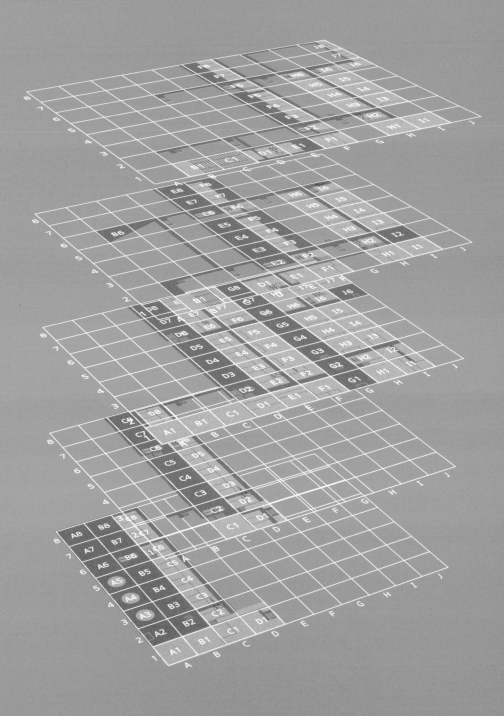

サインのシステムを考えている時、正方形に近い平面のプランを見て、グリッドに割ってみた。すると縦8、横10のグリッドに各階のプランがすっぽりはまる事が分かり、縦＝数字横＝アルファベットの関係で位置を表示した。目的の室名記号からマップ上の位置を確認し、現在位置との関係を知ることができる。

When conceptualizing the sign system, I applied a grid to the near square plans of each stage, and found that all could be accommodated in an 8 x 10 grid. Numbers 1 to 8 were applied to the vertical axes and alphabets to horizontal axes to show the position. Visitors can locate their destinations identified by symbols on the map, and find directions to that point from their present location.

# 4

FLOOR

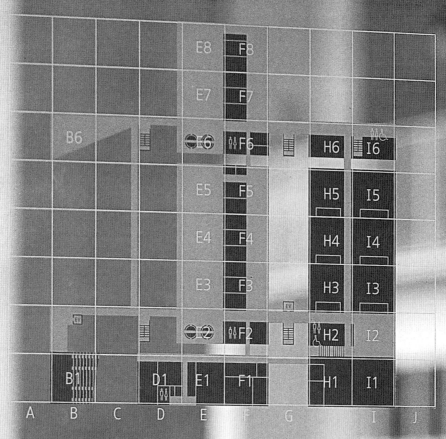

各部屋の位置をアルファベットと数字で表して…

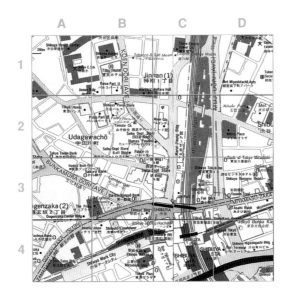

海外の都市マップでもこのＸＹ軸、グリッド方式は良く見かける。ブロックごとに情報がまとめられているので、検索しやすく、距離のスケール感も分かりやすい。グリッドは基本的な造形パターンなので、日本では将棋、囲碁、海外では、チェス、オセロ等、ゲームのフォーマットになっており、思考や創作の起点と呼べる。

This grid-style map with X and Y axes is popular in many cities. It is easy for a user to search a place, and to have an idea of distance. The grid is a basic figurative pattern widely used for Japanese and western chess games, Go, the othello game and so on. It can be the starting point for contemplation and creation.

| 9 | 8 | 7 | 6 | 5 | 4 | 3 | 2 | 1 | |
|---|---|---|---|---|---|---|---|---|---|
| 香 | | | | | | 馬 | 杜 | 香 | 一 |
| | | | 桂 | 銀 | 銀 | 王 | 飛 | | 二 |
| | 歩 | 桂 | | 歩 | 歩 | | 歩 | | 三 |
| 歩 | | 歩 | | 馬 | | 歩 | | 歩 | 四 |
| | | | 歩 | | | | | | 五 |
| 歩 | | 歩 | 歩 | 歩 | 銀 | 歩 | | 歩 | 六 |
| | 歩 | 桂 | 銀 | | 歩 | | 歩 | | 七 |
| | 角 | 金 | | 金 | | 王 | | | 八 |
| 香 | | | | | | | 桂 | 香 | 九 |

建物にはガラスが多く使われており、全体に透明性が高い。授業をガラス箱の中で受けているようなもので、設計段階では、開校しても学生が落ち着かず、授業に集中できないのではないか、という指摘があった。しかし実際には、開放的な環境で、教授と学生の一体感がより強くなり、学科の違う学生が自主的に講義に参加するなどメリットが多かった。外構のサイン計画では矢印を使ったシステムを提案した。細いポールに付く矢印はアウトラインになっており、風景が抜けて見える。矢印に付く影の部分に情報を入れて誘導するのだが、文字の視認性等の問題で実行はできなかった。

Glass is used abundantly for the buildings. Classrooms have high transparency. It is as if students are studying in a glass box and at first, it was feared that they would not be able to concentrate on the lecture. In fact, quite to the contrary, it has had positive influence bringing about changes such as better teacher-student communication in an open atmosphere, and students of other faculties often participated with other classes. For the outdoor sign system in the campus, we proposed an idea to use signposts using arrow marks. The arrows were to be made with a transparent material so that the landscape could be seen, and the information was to be given on the shadowy portions. Due to poor visibility, this proposal was not implemented.

049

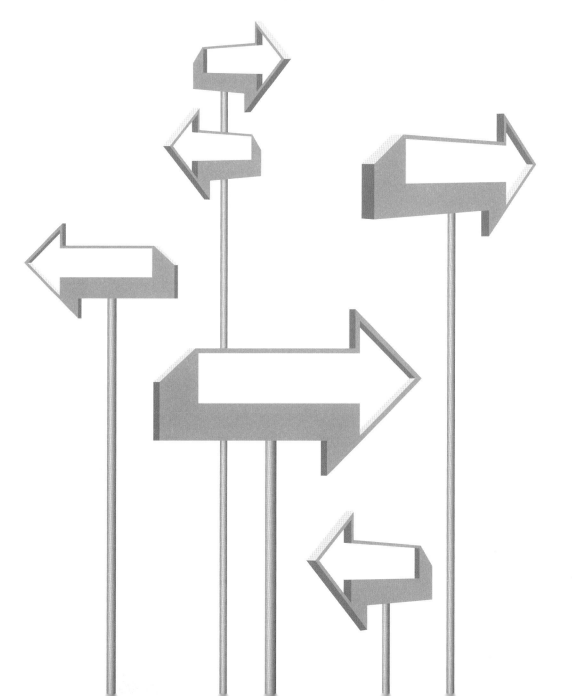

050

グラフィックデザインは理論的には質量がありません。実際の表現では、図形・色彩・記号（文字）の三つの要素で情報を整理・構成し、印刷等の行程を経て第三者へと伝達されます。そのほとんどの表現は、限定された平面の枠の中で完結されるデザインです。質感とか重量といったリアルな条件が希薄な分だけ表現は無限に広がり、想像を超えた映像や多様な色彩の表現が可能となるのです。

一方で、ここでお話しする「空間のグラフィズム」とは、理論的な枠を超えて、単に平面を空間に持ち込むことではなく、空間を視覚的に再構成するというデザイン行為と規定します。さらにいえば、平面的なグラフィックが単に立体化し、手の届く範囲のサイズが拡大化するだけでなく、そのデザインが表現される空間＝環境との関係性に重きをおいて計画していく考え方です。空間が対象となりますから、リアルな質感や重量も重要な条件となります。

サインシステムの場合、環境や空間の目的によっては、必ずしも視認性を最優先しない手法をとることがあります。むしろ、環境と同化させて、サイン自体を意識させない表現が効果的であったり、文字やピクトグラムを用いなくても色彩や質感を設定することでサインの機能を果たすことがあります。つまり、既成概念にとらわれずに、環境との関係性をいかに読み込むかによって、グラフィックの手法やアイデアは決定されるべきだと考えています。

空間を創造する過程にグラフィックデザインが積極的に関わることで、空間全体の目的を明確にし、空間の意味と価値をより高めることに意義があるのです。

Graphic design has no mass theoretically. Without physical properties such as texture or weight, its expression can be expanded indefinitely. Unimaginable images and colors can be expressed. Information is classified, and composed with three graphic elements, figures, colors and symbols (letters), and through the process of printing, it is communicated to the third party. Most graphic designs are completed within a frame on a two dimensional plane.

Graphic designs in a space do not simply mean that they become three-dimensional, and that open-armed dimensions are expanded. At the same time, texture and weight become important factors. More important is the relation of the graphic designs with the environment in which they are placed.

In a sign system, visibility is not always of the utmost priority, depending on where signs are located. Often, it is more important for signs to assimilate with the environment. In other words, they are more effective when their designs are not too conspicuous. Just by slightly hanging their colors and texture, signs can ably function as signs, rather than using letters. The expression and technique for graphics should be determined in consideration of their relations with the environment.

With graphic designs, the purpose of the entire space can be clearly presented. The significance of graphics is that they can add a higher value to the space.

**CM**

### ビッグハート出雲

アートディレクション：廣村正彰
デザイン：廣村正彰、前田豊
建築設計：小島一浩
（シーラカンス アンド アソシエイツ）
家具設計：中村隆秋
ランドスケープ：長谷川浩己
コーディネーション：山崎あかね
施工：ティ・グラバー
クライアント：出雲市

### Big Heart Izumo

art direction : Hiromura Masaaki
design : Hiromura Masaaki,
Maeda Yutaka
architect : Kojima Kazuhiro
(Coelacanth and Associates)
furniture design : Nakamura Takaaki
landscape : Hasegawa Hiromi
coordination : Yamazaki Akane
construction : T·Glover
client : Izumo City

### 東証Arrows

アートディレクション：廣村正彰
デザイン：廣村正彰、水野佳史
内装設計：近藤康夫
総合企画：電通
施工：丹青社
クライアント：東京証券取引所

### Tokyo Stock Exchange Arrows

art direction : Hiromura Masaaki
design : Hiromura Masaaki,
Mizuno Yoshifumi
interior architect : Kondoh Yasuo
plan : Dentsu
construction : Tanseisha
client : Tokyo Stock Exchange

### 名城大学

サインディレクション：廣村正彰、藤田克美
デザイン：廣村正彰、木住野英彰
写真：今井正明
施工：コトブキ
クライアント：名城大学

### Meijo University

sign direction : Hiromura Masaaki,
Fujita Katsumi
design : Hiromura Masaaki,
Kishino Hideaki
photograph : Imai Masaaki
construction : Kotobuki
client : Meijo University

### 東京ウェルズテクニカルセンター

アートディレクション：廣村正彰
デザイン：廣村正彰、前田豊
建築設計：山本理顕
施工：平和建設
クライアント：東京ウェルズ

### Tokyo Weld Technical Center

art direction : Hiromura Masaaki
design : Hiromura Masaaki,
Maeda Yutaka
architect : Yamamoto Riken
construction : Heiwa Construction
client : Tokyo Weld

### CODAN Shinonome 1街区

サインディレクション：廣村正彰
デザイン：廣村正彰、前田豊
建築設計：山本理顕
クライアント：都市基盤整備公団

### Codan Shinonome District 1

sign direction : Hiromura Masaaki
design : Hiromura Masaaki, Maeda Yutaka
architect : Yamamoto Riken
client : Urban Development Corporation

052    BIG HEART IZUMO

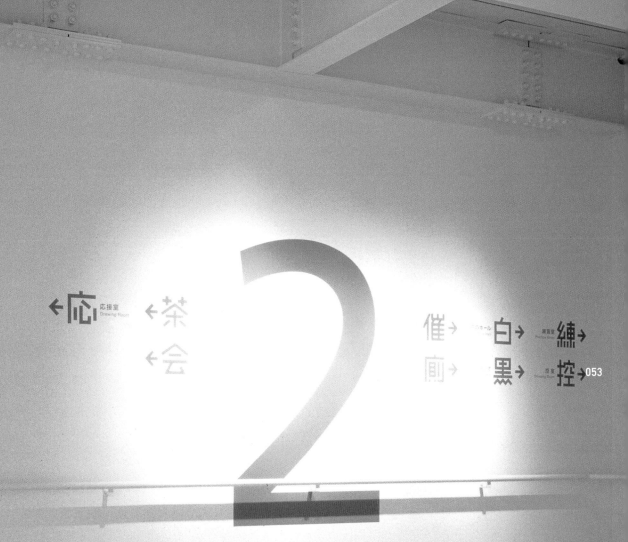

← 応 応接室 Drawing Room　← 茶　← 会

催→ ○○ホール Practice Group　白→ 練習室 繍→

廁→ 黒→ 控室 控→053

島根県出雲市の「ビッグハート出雲」は多目的ホールやギャラリーなど、市民の交流施設として設計された。出雲といえば日本の歴史上重要な神事の場所、出雲大社をはじめ地域全体に厳かなイメージがある。施設の中にあるホールやスタジオには当初から白、黒、茶と漢字の名称が付けられていたこともあり、地域性も考えて漢字を中心にしたサインシステムを提案した。

This was designed as a cultural facility for Izumo citizens with multi-purpose hall and a gallery. Izumo is one of the important historic and Shinto religious centers. The Izumo Grand Shrine and the entire city give a solemn image. The hall, studios and other rooms were given names such as White, Black, Brown and so on in Chinese characters. Therefore, we designed the sign system using Chinese characters as the main motif.

mountain

cloud

leaf

river

人類は意志を伝えるための手段として文字を発明した。まず表情や身振りによる表現から、音声による言語に発達し、言葉の概念が絵画の手法により、記号としての文字に改良された。絵文字から象形（ヒエログリフ）へ、そして文字が意味をもつ表意（イデオグラフ）へ発達する。これが漢字の原点になる。その昔日本は独自の文字を持っていなかった。日本語を表記するために日本人が初めて使ったのは、隣の中国で使われていた漢字である。その後日本人は漢字を変化させたカナを発明し、現在に至るまで漢字とカナの組み合わせを日本語として使用している。アルファベットと違い一字で意味を表す漢字は、ピクトグラムと匹敵する記号化の表現である。ただ画数の多い文字は視認性が悪くなるので、なるべく大きく表現することができれば、今回のこの施設に相応しい考え方だと思いサインシステムを漢字一字で表現することにチャレンジした。

horse

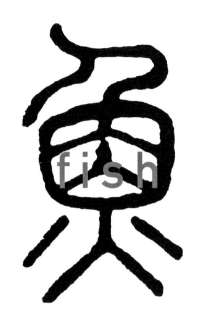

fish

mouse

bird

Humans invented characters as a means to communicate with others. From facial expressions and gestures, languages using voices were developed, and the concept of language was symbolized with the method of drawing pictures, or pictorial symbols. From here, hieroglyphs were devices followed by ideograph, which is the origin of Chinese characters. Chinese characters, each showing meaning, can compare with pictograms. I thought of creating the sign system by using one Chinese character for every facility. As some characters with many strokes have lower visibility, we would have to use large letters. Japan did not have letters. The first characters that the Japanese used to describe the Japanese language were Chinese characters imported from neighboring China. Later, the Japanese invented two kinds of Kana, phonetic signs, and have used the combination of Chinese characters and Kana.

文字はその表現方法により、ずいぶん違ったイメージを与えるものである。漢字でサインシステムを考えた場合、この建築のプランはとても革新的でモダンなので、表現する漢字のグラフィックは、歴史的に重要な地域性をふまえ、現代から未来に向け、これまで以上に進化発展する意味を込めて、本来漢字のイメージである筆文字や明朝ではなく、ソリッドでデザイン的に、すべて直線で創作した。

Letters give different images by styles. As the architectural plan was modern and innovative, we designed Chinese characters using only straight lines instead of the usual calligraphic style, wishing that this historic locality would continue to develop into the future.

黒のスタジオ
Black Studio

057

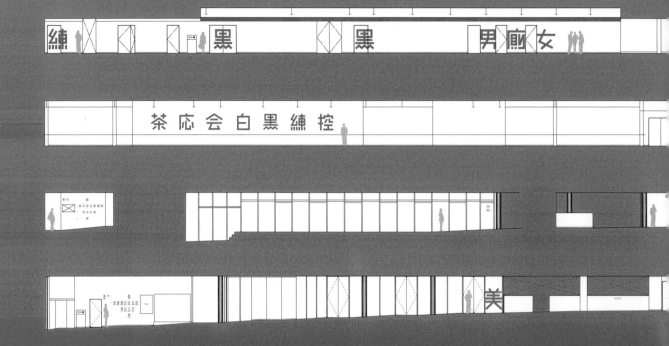

サインシステムは2案考えた。漢字のプランともう一つは、誘導と表示が壁面に水平のラインで記されているもの。この建物は1階の中心部分が意図的に隆起しており、小山のある公園に建築が乗っているイメージである。人々が1階を自由に行き来し、起伏を感じることで意識的に施設と関わっ

てもらうことを期待している。壁面のラインは、なだらかな起伏を感じるための視覚的な仕掛けであり、誘導や上下階の施設の位置関係を知るツールになる。建築設計の小島一浩さんは少し考えてから、漢字のプランを選択されたが、主張の強いサインと建築とのバランスに悩まれたのだろう。

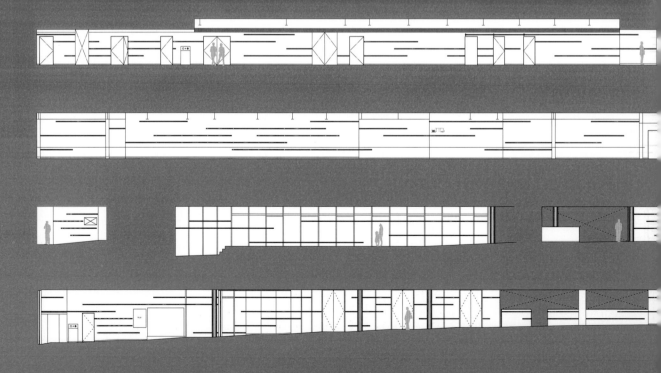

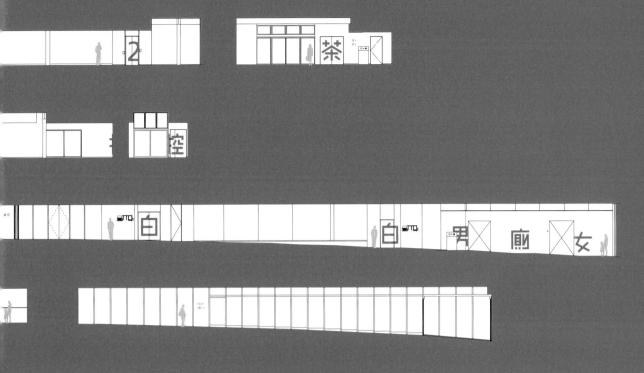

We prepared two draft sign systems, the Chinese character system and the other in which guidelines and destinations were horizontally expressed on the corridor walls. The central part of the ground floor raised intentionally, as if the building is built on a small mountain in a park. Architect Kojima Kazuhiro expects that the visitors will have a closer association with the building by walking up and down the floor. The horizontal signboards on the walls will help visitors become aware of the gentle slope of the floor, and know the facilities on upper and lower floors. After some thought, the architect chose the Chinese character system. He may have been puzzled over the balance between the building and strongly appealing signs.

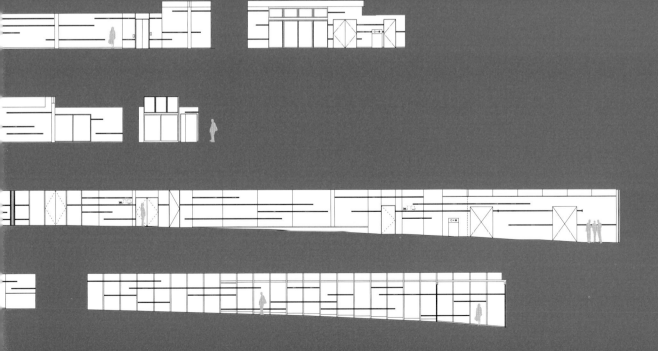

白
白のホール
White Hall

黒
黒のスタジオ
Black Studio

茶
茶のスタジオ
Brown Studio

会
会議室
Conference Room

応
応接室
Drawing Room

受
受付
Information

文
文化サロン
Culture Salon

美
アートギャラリー
Art Gallery

練
練習室
Practice Room

控
控室
Dressing Room

催
レセプション
Reception

食
レストラン
Restaurant

駐
駐車場
Parking

輪
駐輪場
Bicycle

煙
喫煙所
Smoking Area

廁
化粧室
Toilets

男
化粧室
Toilets

女
化粧室
Toilets

電
電話
Telephone

搬
搬入口
Back Entrance

建物内の施設、室名は全て漢字一文字で表記した。総合案内も階数ごとに室名の漢字をまとめ、壁面全体を透過性のシートで被い、内照式にしている。建築家や出雲市の方々にはサインの主旨をとても良く理解していただいたが、竣工後「厠-かわや」の表記だけは、現在では一般的でなく認知しずらいとのことで変更をした。

Every facility within the building is expressed with a single Chinese character. The general information board collects the characters indicating the facilities on each floor. The board is covered with a transparent sheet and lit from inside. The architects and people of the city liked the signboard. Later, however, it was found that the Chinese character for "toilet" was not popular among young people, and this particular letter was replaced.

サイン計画の場合、実際に設置するまでに何度も現場を観察する。空間の感覚を肌で感じ、建築素材の確認、目線での距離感などを体感しながら、原寸大のサインサンプルを実際の場所に貼ってみる。コピーペーパーを貼り合わせて作った大きな漢字を現場に持っていくと、作業中の人が手を止めて興味を示してくれる。現場でのコミュニケーションは重要な情報源でもある。

We visited the actual site to place signboards a number of times. We applied the real size samples to the place, feeling the space, confirming the construction materials, and measuring the distances between the sign and visitors. When we were pasting the large copies of Chinese characters, people working for the construction stopped their work and showed their interest in our signs. We obtained good hints through communicating with these people.

066    TOKYO STOCK EXCHANGE ARROW

東京証券取引所は、株式売買をいままでの立会場での人手による方法から、市場情報の発信および投資家と上場企業の交流を主な目的とする施設に変わった。従来の活気ある立会いが消え、寂しい感じもするが、世界的なIT化に対応する為に改変した。しかし株式市場のシンボルであることには変わりがない。中心となるマーケットセンターは透明なガラスシリンダーで設計され、メディアを通して株式情報を全国に発信している。

Stock dealing at the Tokyo Stock Exchange is now fully computerized replacing the traditional trading by finger signs at the boardroom. It now serves as a facility to give market information, and to promote communication between investors and listed companies. As the symbolic entity, the Market Center is designed as a glass cylinder through which stock market information is transmitted by TV every day.

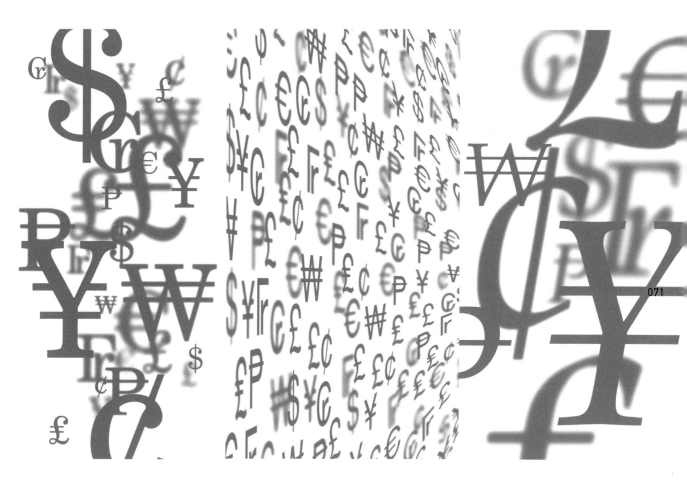

2階の見学ロビーの東証プラザは、証券取引に関する知識を紹介する場である。ここには検索モニターがセットされた光る柱が9本あり、証券をはじめ、為替などのイメージを数字や記号のグラフィックで表現し、それぞれの柱を内照式で設置するというプレゼンテーションをしてみた。しかしこのプランは残念ながら却下された。企業が株式上場の時、パーティ等に使用する為、固定的なイメージを持たせたくないというのが理由であった。

The TSE Plaza in the visitors' lobby on the 2nd floor gives information about stock exchange. We first planned to install 9 pillars with built-in computer terminals for searching, to apply graphics in the images of stock, foreign exchange, numerals and symbols on these pillars and to illuminate them from inside. Unfortunately, this idea was turned down, because this space would be used for parties for companies listing their stocks for the first time, and the TSE did not want to give a fixed image to this space.

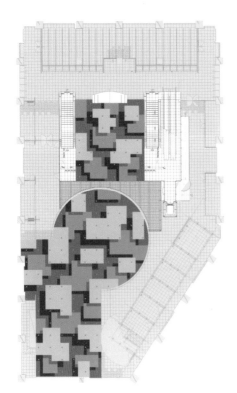
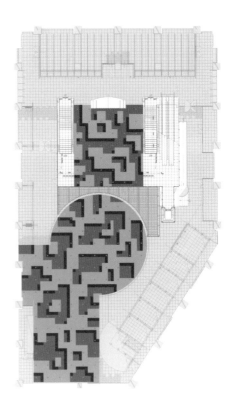

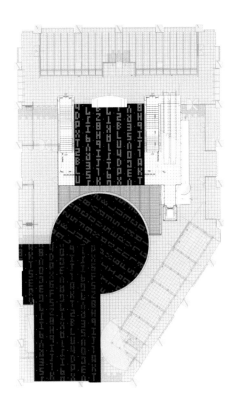

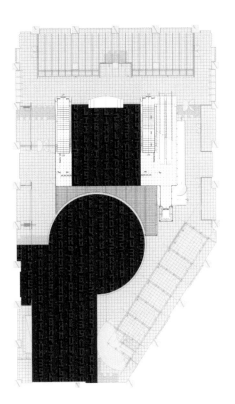

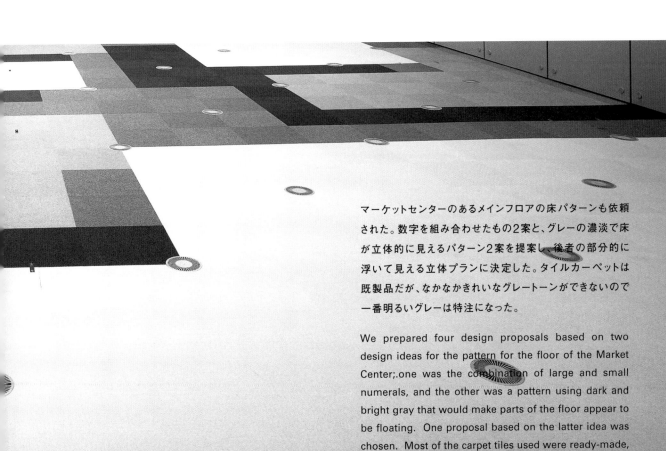

マーケットセンターのあるメインフロアの床パターンも依頼された。数字を組み合わせたもの2案と、グレーの濃淡で床が立体的に見えるパターン2案を提案し、後者の部分的に浮いて見える立体プランに決定した。タイルカーペットは既製品だが、なかなかきれいなグレートーンができないので一番明るいグレーは特注になった。

We prepared four design proposals based on two design ideas for the pattern for the floor of the Market Center;.one was the combination of large and small numerals, and the other was a pattern using dark and bright gray that would make parts of the floor appear to be floating. One proposal based on the latter idea was chosen. Most of the carpet tiles used were ready-made, but we had to tailor the brightest gray carpet tiles.

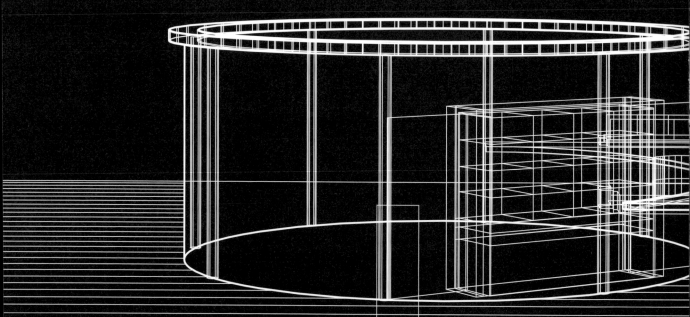

3階には見学者が上部より観覧できる回廊があり、施設を詳しく説明するサインが必要になった。設計の近藤康夫さんと相談して、ガラス越しに見下ろすので、通常であればガラス面にサインを取り付けるのだが、ガラスとは反対の壁面全体を使い、ラインで構成したグラフィックで施設の機能を説明するサインにした。

There is a cloister on the 3rd floor for the visitors to observe the Stock Market through glass windows from above. Signs to give detailed explanation about the facility were required. Consulting with the architect Kondoh Yasuo, we decided to use the whole space of the walls opposite to the glass windows to explain the functions of the facility with graphics composed with lines.

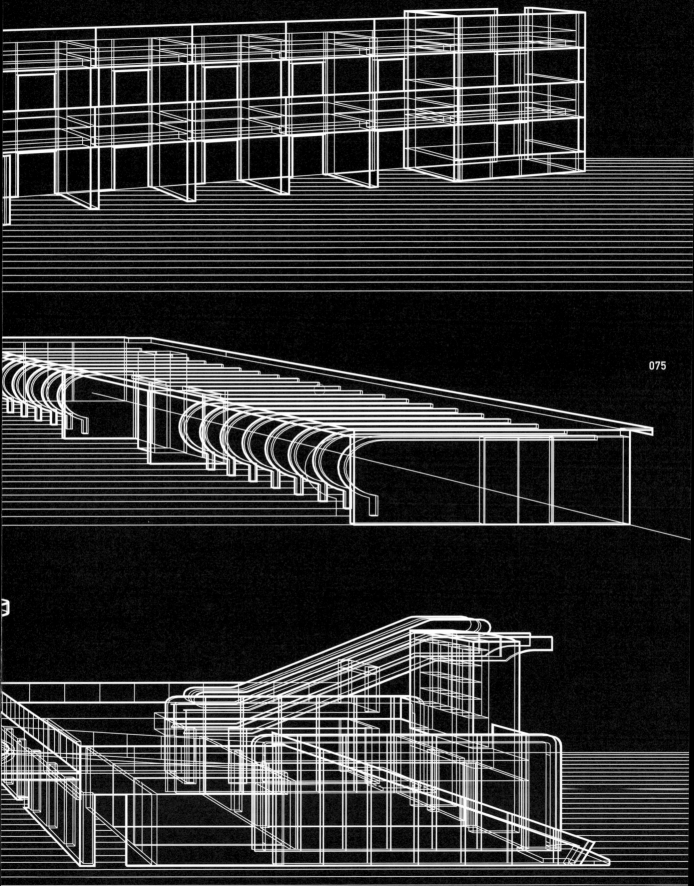

076

回廊は改装の予定はなかったが、サインのプランに基づき、天井と壁を黒く塗装し、内側のガラスから入ってくる光で照度が取れるように設定した。ちょうど映画館の中を歩きながらスクリーンを眺めている感覚に似ているので、見学者も集中できて、距離の疲労を感じない。

To coordinate with the sign plan, the ceiling and walls of the cloister were repainted in black, so that incoming light from the glass can be used as lighting. It was like watching a movie screen while walking in an isle of a theater. The visitors would concentrate on viewing, and would not feel that the cloister has a long length.

ワイアーフレームで作ったグラフィックを壁面に表示する方
法を検討した結果、カッティングシートを選択。何回か現場
で原寸の物を貼ってテストを行ったが、壁に転写する際に
水を使うので、細いラインが逃げてしまい失敗だった。線を
太くし、クロスする線も加えて実現した。

After attempting to display graphics made of wire
frames on the wall, we chose to use stencils. We tried
to transfer graphics to the wall, but failed because we
used water to transfer the graphics and because of
this, fine lines were blurred. Then, we drew bolder
lines and crossing lines to add dynamism.

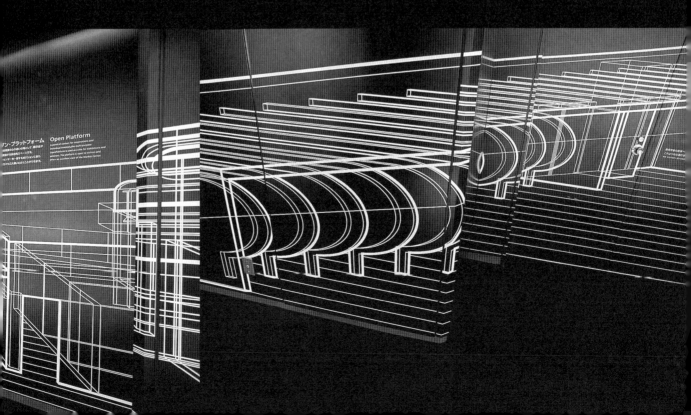

## 今こそ、予測不能なコラボレートを

## 近藤康夫 ✕ 廣村正彰

空間のグラフィックデザイン

近藤：正直なところ、世のグラフィックデザイナーの多くは平面の世界から抜け出せ
ない人が多いように思います。興味もあるし、実際に手掛けている方も多数いますが、
空間という広がりが見えていないような気がする。ロゴをつくる場合でも、ショッピン
グバッグやタグ、ステーショナリーへの展開としては素晴らしいものであっても、それ
が店の空間展開にまで考えが及びながらデザインしている人は残念ながらなかなか
いないんですね。

廣村：確かに、平面であるがゆえの限界はあるような気がします。グラフィックデザイ
ナーが捉えている空間デザインの認識は、単純に平面の拡張である場合が多い。簡
単に言えば80年代に流行ったスーパー・グラフィック。建物の壁に巨大な絵を掛け
るとか、巨大なサインを付けるといったものを空間のグラフィックとして捉えていた節
がありますが、実は、あれはひとつの切り取られたグラフィックの手法であって、空間
のデザインとして距離感や人間の目線にまで踏み込むような立体的なデザインでは
有り得なかったからです。僕は、本来、デザイナーというものはグラフィックに限らず、
もっと守備範囲が広がっていったほうがいいのではないかと思います。

近藤：グラフィックというのは意識してみる世界ですよね。ビジュアルとか視覚伝達と
言われるとおり、人が注視して見るようにする、情報伝達のデザインだと思う。常に見
る側が意識するので常に近景となる。ところが空間は、そこにただ「ある」という形な
んです。中景も遠景も近景もある。遠景では「何かがそこにある」という程度に見え
ていたサインも、中景になるとどういう認識をされるようになり、最終的に近づいた時
にはどのような情報が伝わるか、さまざまな関係がある。しかも、時間やシーンによっ
ても変化する。だからスケール感というもの自体が、壁面とのプロポーションやバラ
ンスだけでは図れない、多様な広がりのあるものになるわけです。

廣村：関係性で成り立っているものなんでしょう。対してグラフィックというのは単体
で成り立っていて、常に相対的なんですよ。だから限られたスペースにおいて表現す
ることが多いため、そういう意味では「空間」という概念では距離感はあるかもしれな
い。ただ、サインデザインなど、今後、空間にグラフィックデザイナーが関わっていくこ
とを考えてみた場合、誘導とか名称の認知といった機能的な部分だけではなく、空間
を演出するといった役割になるのではないでしょうか。そうすると「サインデザイン」と
いうより、これからは「空間のグラフィックをやる」と認識したほうがいいというのが僕
の実感です。

| Collaboration that produces unpredictable results |
| Kondoh Yasuo × Hiromura Masaaki |

Graphic Designs for Spaces

Kondoh: It is unfortunate that many graphic designers are not able to get out of the two-dimensional world. Many are interested in and are actually working for spaces, but I don't feel that they are seeing the expanse of a space. The logos they design are very good for shopping bags, tags and stationery, but I can hardly find logos that are designed with the consideration that they are going to be used in a shop.

Hiromura: Certainly, I feel that there is a limit as a two-dimensional designer. Graphic designers often see space design simply as an extension of two-dimensional design. Super graphics were in fashion during the 1980s and large illustrations or signs were hung on the outside walls of buildings. They seemed to have considered that these were graphic designs for spaces. In fact, they were a part of graphic expression but they did not present feelings of distance, or they were not designed considering the viewers' line of vision. I feel that designers of any genre should have a wider coverage beyond their specialization.

Kondoh: People see graphics with consciousness. As they are said to be "visual communication tools," they are intended to cause people to look attentively. So, they are always meant to be seen from a short distance. On the other hand, graphics in spaces are something that can be seen "over there." They are seen from a medium distance or long distance. A sign which is just seen as "There is something over there" from a distance can become visible and recognized as a viewer comes closer, and finally it gives some information. There are various relations between a sign and a viewer. A sign may change according to time and scenes. The sense of scale can be expanded in many ways besides considering its proportion and balance with the wall space.

Hiromura: Because relativity matters in space design, while graphics are independent and expressed in one limited surface. But if graphic designers are going to be more involved in designing for spaces, we will become more concerned about designing a space itself in addition to the functions of signs to guide visitors and to show the names of the buildings. It may be better that we understand our work to be, not just designing signs independently, but that "we design graphics for spaces."

空間を捉えるスケール感

近藤：実際に、廣村さんはそういう視点から仕事をしているじゃないですか。

廣村：そうしたいと考えているんです。ただ文字だ、矢印だということに終始するのではなく、空間に対してグラフィカルに考える、グラフィックデザインがどういう役割を果たしていくのかを探っていければいいなと思う。

近藤：きっとそういう意識があったから、岩出山中学校が生まれたんだと思う。あれは新鮮だったし、かなりの遠景として見ても存在感があるところがすごい。単にロゴタイプとしての数字や文字のプレートがついているだけだったら近景にしかなりませんからね。あれは単なる「サイン」としてではなく展開されている数字だということが一目でわかる。

廣村：あの当時は環境や建築と同化するサインを心掛けていたんです。空間に後付けの情報として貼り付けるだけのサインではなく、もっと建築や空間と同化できるものをと考えていました。その後、なにも無理やりに建築と同化することが良いことだと限らないと思いはじめて、限定して考えないほうがむしろ自然ではないかという結論に至りました。最近は「空間のグラフィック」を考えるほうが自然じゃないだろうかとなって、それで近藤さんとご一緒した「東京証券取引所」も、その観点から展開しています。

近藤：床を意識し始めたのもそのせいなのでしょうか。

廣村：廊下に施した、ラインだけでつくった絵柄というのは、ある意味、サインとしてはあまり機能していません。つまり情報の集約になっていませんが、訪れた人がヴィジュアルを意識することで、情報を受け取るための心構えができる、そういうツールとして機能しているのです。象徴された図柄による、ある種の誘導的な役割が、あの場合のグラフィックには大きい。だから、床も壁と同じように何かに使える場所と考えています。

近藤：「空間のデザイン」と言った時に、重要なのはスケール感を把握できるかどうかだと思う。廣村さんは、今まで一緒に仕事をした他のグラフィックデザイナーたちに比べて格段にスケール感があるし、こちらのイメージをわかってもらえると感じます。それは仕事で得た実体験が経験値として蓄積されているせいかもしれないし、あるいはそもそもの感性なのかもしれないし、それはわかりませんが、とにかく、そこから何が出てくるのかが面白い。

グラフィックという可能性

廣村：現実として、空間におけるグラフィックの役割が社会の中で求められはじめているのではないか。そういう類の仕事の量が増えてきているのも事実です。もともとグラフィックデザインというカテゴリー自体が非常に曖昧なんですよ。ブック、パッケ

The sense of scale to conceive a space

Kondoh: You are already working with that standpoint.

Hiromura: I want to do that. Instead of being concerned about letters and arrows, I attempt to conceive a space graphically. I consider what roles graphic designs should play in one particular space.

Kondoh: Because you have this consciousness, the Iwadeyama Junior High School was created in such an impressive way. The school shows its presence from afar. If it had an ordinary logotype and a name plate, the signs would be recognized only at a close distance. The numerical signs of this school can be recognized not only as signs but also as figures that have meaning from a distance.

Hiromura: At that time, I was more conscious about assimilation with the surrounding settings and buildings in designing signs. Later, I came to think that assimilation is not always good, and realized I should not limit myself to some particular concept. Recently, I think that "graphics for spaces" is more natural. So, I designed the Tokyo Stock Exchange from this viewpoint.

Kondoh: Is it the reason why you became conscious about the floor?

Hiromura: Any patterns composed only of lines applied on the floor do not function well as signs. If the floor signs are graphically designed, and if visitors become conscious that they give information, then, they are prepared to see them as information signs. Symbolic patterns have a guiding function in the Stock Exchange building. So, I think that a floor can be used for information purposes just like walls.

Kondoh: What is necessary in designing spaces is whether a designer has an understanding about scale. You have an outstanding sense of scale, and good understanding about what I imagine for my design. You might have accumulated experiences in working for space, or you might have a gifted sense of scale. Whichever it may be, it is intriguing what ideas emerge from you.

Potentiality of graphics

Hiromura: It may be that graphics for spaces are increasingly demanded. As a matter of fact, the volume of my work to design graphics for spaces is on the rise. The borders of graphic design with other design categories are ambiguous. It goes into books, packages, advertisements, CI, signs and other genres. Graphic designs are needed in a wide range of designs.

ージ、広告、CI、サインといろいろなジャンルに入り込んで、さまざまなデザインをしているのがグラフィックですし、むしろそうした中途半端なカテゴリーであること自体がグラフィックらしさであり、広範囲に求められていることではないかと思う。

近藤：ところが、これまでの現状としてはグラフィックはある種閉じたカテゴリーとされていたように見える。

**廣村：そういう気はします。なぜなのかは不思議ですが。**

近藤：広告というキーワードのもとに閉鎖した世界を確立できてしまったということではないですか。元来、いろいろなジャンルとコラボレーションすべきカテゴリーであるはずなのに、そうしないで縦割りのカテゴリーで閉じることのできる条件や背景が存在していた。ところが、世の中の意識や要求が広がってきて、廣村さんのような人々が徐々に気付きはじめたというのが今なのかもしれない。

**廣村：グラフィックデザイナーの人たちの多くは、建築やインテリアなどの空間に関して大いに興味を持っています。とは言え、その興味が実際に空間に関わる仕事へ直結するということにはなり得ません。そうした状況だからこそ、空間をデザインする人々とグラフィックの人がコラボレーションをしていくいいチャンスなんですよ。**

最終形のないリクエスト

近藤：実は、コラボレーションをするには、今は、私にとっても非常にいい段階でもある。というのは、私は空間をデザインするに際して、自分なりの空間を把握するための方程式を組み立てて、仕事をしてきました。つまりは、自分自身の仕事の流れとしての段階です。簡単にいうと、これまでの自分のインテリアデザインを分類していくと数段階に分けることができる。第一段階は空間の「構成」そのものを構築しようとした時代。第二段階は「形」を追求した時代で、かなり派手な作品群を排出しました。第三段階では表情的なニュアンスを排除して、機械のような直喩的な表現をめざしました。その次に色や素材などの変化によってニュアンスや表情を取り入れていく第四段階があって、今、廣村さんと組むようになってめざしているのは次の段階なんです。

**廣村：巨大なビルのワンフロアを、とにかく床だけやってくれ、という話になるということでしょうか。タイルカーペットを使うという条件のみで、「ゾーニングも何も関係ない」と言われましたが。**

近藤：「ここにこういうブースが来て、こうなります」という最終形態があった上でデザインをしてくれと頼むべきところを、「上に何がくるか全然考えないで、床だけやって欲しい」とお願いするという、まさにそういうことです。極端に言えば、できてみないとどういう見え方をするのかはわからない、そういうコラボレーション。

**廣村：あの仕事では全部数字にして、ダーッと並べました。あれは楽しかった。**

近藤：変な話かもしれませんが、全部自分で決めるよりはいろいろな人に関わっても

Kondoh: But, so far, graphic design has been closed into one design category.

Hiromura: Yes. I wonder why it is.

Kondoh: It might have established itself within a limited circle of advertisement. Graphic designers should work together with designers of different genres. But until now graphic designers could work alone within this sector of design. And now, people's consciousness and desire have changed. And people like you have noticed the need for collaboration with designers of other genres.

Hiromura: Many graphic designers are interested in architecture, and interior, but their interest rarely is linked to their works. It is now time for space designers and graphic designers to collaborate.

Design process without the image of the end result

Kondoh: It is good timing for me to work in collaboration with other designers. I have worked with my own formula to design spaces. Looking back on my past works, I can divide them into four phases. At the beginning, I attempted to "build" the structure of a building itself. The second was the time when I pursued "forms" and I designed quite showy interior works. In the third phase, I pursued direct, mechanical expressions and in the fourth phase, I attempted to express different nuances by the variation of colors and materials. Now, I am intending to go into the fifth phase as a result of having worked together with you.

Hiromura: Do you mean that you will give me an order to design the floor of a gigantic building with only the given conditions of using tile carpets and no other conditions for zoning or anything?

Kondoh: Instead of saying "Here comes a booth of so-and-so shape of so and so size," the client will say "Please do not consider what we put on the floor, but just design the floor." Yes, it means this way. If I put it in an extreme way, you cannot tell how the floor will look like until the work is finished. This is the kind of collaboration I want.

Hiromura: In that Stock Exchange project, we arranged everything in figures, and I enjoyed it very much.

Kondoh: It may sound funny, but what I am trying to do is to involve many people, and destroy what I had planned. I think something new will come out from such destruction. I am thinking to stop constructing a thing exactly as planned.

らってグチャグチャにして、最後にどういうものができるか。それが今、僕のめざしている段階なんです。自分の考えと寸分違わずずれないようにと緻密に構築することをやめようとしている。

互いに領域と意識を超えて

廣村：普通、建築やインテリアの方から依頼を受ける場合は、スペースの条件や目的、機能などの必要条件以外に「こういうものをやってほしい」というイメージのニュアンスが伝わってきます。ところが近藤さんの場合は、スペースと目的がある他は「あとは宜しく」という感じで、ニュアンスがほとんど伝わってこない。僕としては「どうすればいいの？」というところから始まることになり、提案する時にはまるで賭けをしているような感じになる。期待以上のものに仕上がるのか、期待を裏切るか、二つに一つという感じ。

近藤：吉と出るか凶と出るか、できてみないとわからないというのがいいんです。予定調和じゃつまらないし、そもそもコラボレーションの意味がない。

廣村：確かに、コラボレーションの面白さはこういうところにあるのかもしれません。

近藤：コラボレーションは生き物なんです。相手を裏切らないと面白くない。それができれば、グラフィックだ、インテリアだといった領域を結果的に超えることができる。ほどほどのものをほどほどに合わせるという単なる異業種間の共同作業に終わらせるのではなく、意識をどれだけ超えられるかということが重要なのであって、枠組みに嵌める必要はまったくない。

廣村：求められた、その上を超えるものを出すこと、なるべく裏切ることを考えています。技術的なことに囚われることなく、「できたらいいな」という観点でやっていくということも含めて。

近藤：歳も立場的にも近いところがあるし、いろいろ共通項はあるけれど、だからといって妥協をせずに裏切り、裏切られ続ける関係でありたい。それができなくなれば一緒にやる意味がなくなる。それこそまさしくコラボレーションの面白さですよ。

廣村：想像を絶する「裏切り」をしたいです。

近藤康夫　インテリア・アーキテクト
1950年東京都生まれ。東京造形大学造形学部デザイン学科室内建築専攻修了後、三輪正弘環境造形研究所入社。77年クラマタデザイン事務所入社。81年近藤康夫デザイン事務所設立。88年日本インテリアデザイナー協会協会賞、89年AGB国際インテリアデザイン大賞、00年度毎日デザイン賞等受賞。代表作に「東証 ARROWS」、「Cassina INTER-DECOR」、「YOHJI YAMAMOTO」、「Y's」、「宮城県立図書館」（家具）他。著書に『インテリア・スペース・デザイニング』（グラフィック社刊）がある。

Hiromura: When I work for architects or interior designers, they give me explanations about the space, conditions, purpose and functions of the spaces. And usually they give me their own image of the end products saying "I would like to have something like this, or that." But when I worked with you, you just said something about the space and its purpose, and no other information was conveyed to me. It was like you said, "I leave it with you entirely." So my work begins with "What shall I do?" When I present my idea, it is almost like gambling. Whether my idea is more than you have expected, or it may disappoint you.

Kondoh: Whether it turns out to be fortunate of misfortunate, we cannot know until the construction is completed. It will not be interesting at all if we know the result beforehand, and collaboration has no meaning.

Hiromura: Certainly, that might be an intriguing part of collaboration.

Kondoh: Collaboration is an interactive process. It is not interesting unless we outwit the other. While doing so, we can easily cross over design categories. What is important is how designers can expand our consciousness beyond one's usual frame of reference. Collaboration is not simply a joint work by designers of different genres to apply a moderate graphic design to a moderate interior design.

Hiromura: I attempt to present something that will outwit a given assignment. I will not be too much concerned about technical matters, though I will think that I wish I could do this and that.

Kondoh: Both of us are close in age and positions and have other common points, but I don't want to compromise with you easily. I would like to see if we can continue trying to outwit each other, because this is the most interesting point in collaboration. If we do not keep this attitude, there is no meaning to collaborate.

Hiromura: I would also like to outwit you in an unimagined way.

Kondoh Yasuo, interior architect

Born in Tokyo in 1950. After completing Interior Design Program, Design Department, Tokyo Zokei University, entered Miwa Masahiro Environmental Design Institute. In 1977, employed by Kuramata Design Office. In 1981, established Kondoh Yasuo Design Office. Received the Award of the Japan Interior Designers Association in 1988, AGB International Interior Design Grand Prix in 1989, and Mainichi Design Award in 2000. Major works include "Tokyo Stock Exchange, Arrows," "Cassina Inter-Décor," "Yohji Yamamoto," "Y's," and "Miyagi Prefectural Library" (furniture). Authored *Interior Space Designing* (Graphic-sha Publishing).

2

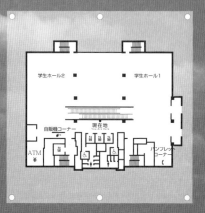

名古屋の名城大学は創立75周年を記念して新校舎を増築、それに伴い、サイン計画のコンペティションが開かれた。名古屋市郊外の丘陵に位置するキャンパスは、周りの環境がとても良く、比較的新しく開発された街並である。開学当時のこの地域はほとんど雑木林であったことは容易に想像がつき、大学を中心に開発が始まったのだろう。

In commemoration of its 75th anniversary, Meijo University in Nagoya built a new school building. The sign system design for this building was put in open competition. The campus is located on the hilly suburbs of Nagoya. The vicinity maintains a thicket of various trees with relatively new town districts. It is easily understood that the area has been developed around the university.

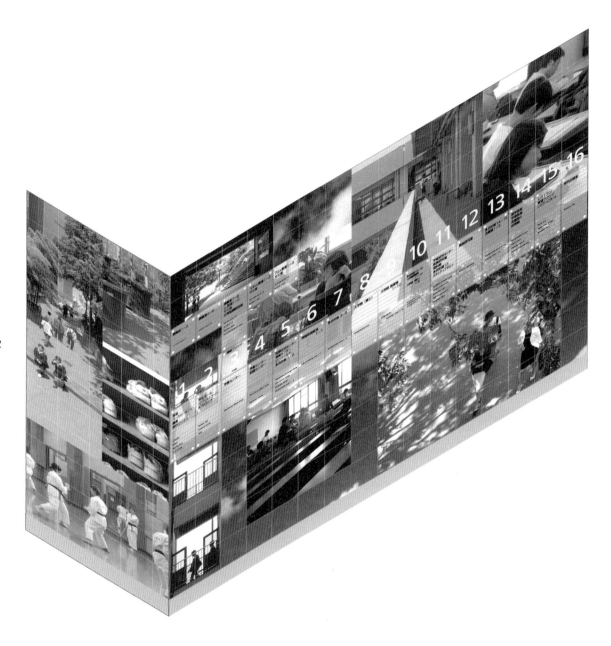

提案したサインシステムのテーマは「記憶」である。70年に渡り、多くの卒業生を排出したこの学舎は、ここで過ごした学生達に重要な時間の記憶を刷り込んでいるはずである。新しく建てられる校舎には、「今」を記録し、定着することで、未来に向けて「記憶」を視覚的に蓄積させたいという願いがある。

The theme for our sign system proposal was "memories." In its more than 70 years, the university must have given many memories to the students who had spent their youthful days here. We wanted to imprint "now" to the new building, so that the memory of today will be engraved to recall in the future.

| 講義室1−3 | 講義室4−6 | 講義室7−8<br>LL教室1−2<br>ゼミ室<br>非常勤講師控室 | 100人教室1−3<br>ゼミ室 | 70人教室1−3<br>ゼミ室 | | | |
|---|---|---|---|---|---|---|---|
| Lecture room 1-3 | Lecture room 4-6 | Lecture room 7-8<br>LL room 1-2<br>Seminar room<br>Part-time lecturer's room | 100' Classroome 1-3<br>Seminar room | 70' Classroome 1-3<br>Seminar room | | | |

連絡ブリッジ
Bridge

# 1 2 3 4 5 6 7 8

| 食堂<br>ベーカリーカフェ<br>購買<br>旅行コーナー | 学生ホール<br>パンフレットコーナー<br>ATMコーナー | 学務センター | 学務センター<br>就職センター | 国際交流センター<br>情報センター<br>エクステンションセンター<br>多目的室 1・2 | 情報処理教室<br>1−7 | 多目的室 3−9 | 大学院（修士） | 093<br>大学院 演習室<br>1− |
|---|---|---|---|---|---|---|---|---|
| Cafeteria<br>Bakery<br>Supplies store<br>Travel Corner | Student Hall<br>Brochure Corner<br>ATM | educational affairs Center | educational affairs Center<br><br>Placement Center | International Exchange Center<br>Information Center<br>Extension Center<br>Multipurpose room 1・2 | Date processing room 1−7 | Multipurpose room 3−9 | Postgraduate room | Postgraduate<br><br>workshop ro |

**Postgraduate workshop room 1**

**Law school Dean's room**

**Multipurpose room 1**

← 3F 高層棟
**Educational affairs center**

具体的には写真表現を中心にしたサインシステムを考えた。全体を大きく三つのグループに分け、一つは現在のキャンパス風景を部分的に切り取り、講義室とか研究室の出入口の壁面に写真表現をする。二つ目はエレベーターとエスカレーターの縦導線に対応した各階の案内で、16階建ての新校舎の屋上から眺める街並と空を、季節と時間別に表現する。三つ目はこの地域に残る貴重な自然を、棟と棟を結ぶ場所に表現し、機能と情報を調和させた。

The use of photos for the sign system was conceived. The signs were divided into three groups. For the first group, parts of the present campus were photographed, and placed at the walls besides entrances to lecture rooms and research rooms. The second group was floor guides along the elevators and escalators. The photos of the townscapes and the skies viewed from the roof of the new building in different seasons and at different times were used. For the third group showing the functions of buildings, the photos of the precious nature remaining in this area were used at the places between two buildings.

# TOKYO WELD TECHNICAL CENTER

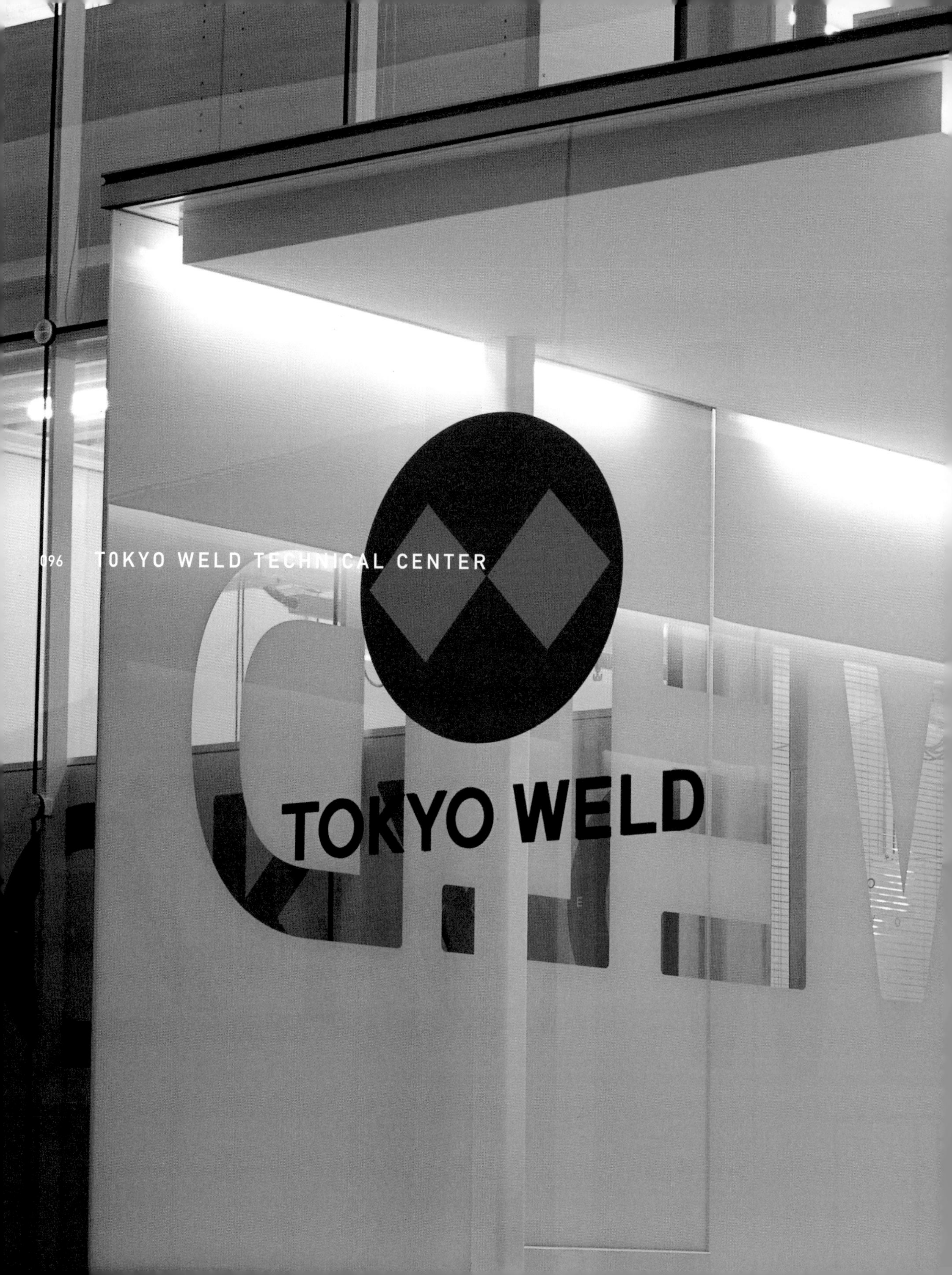

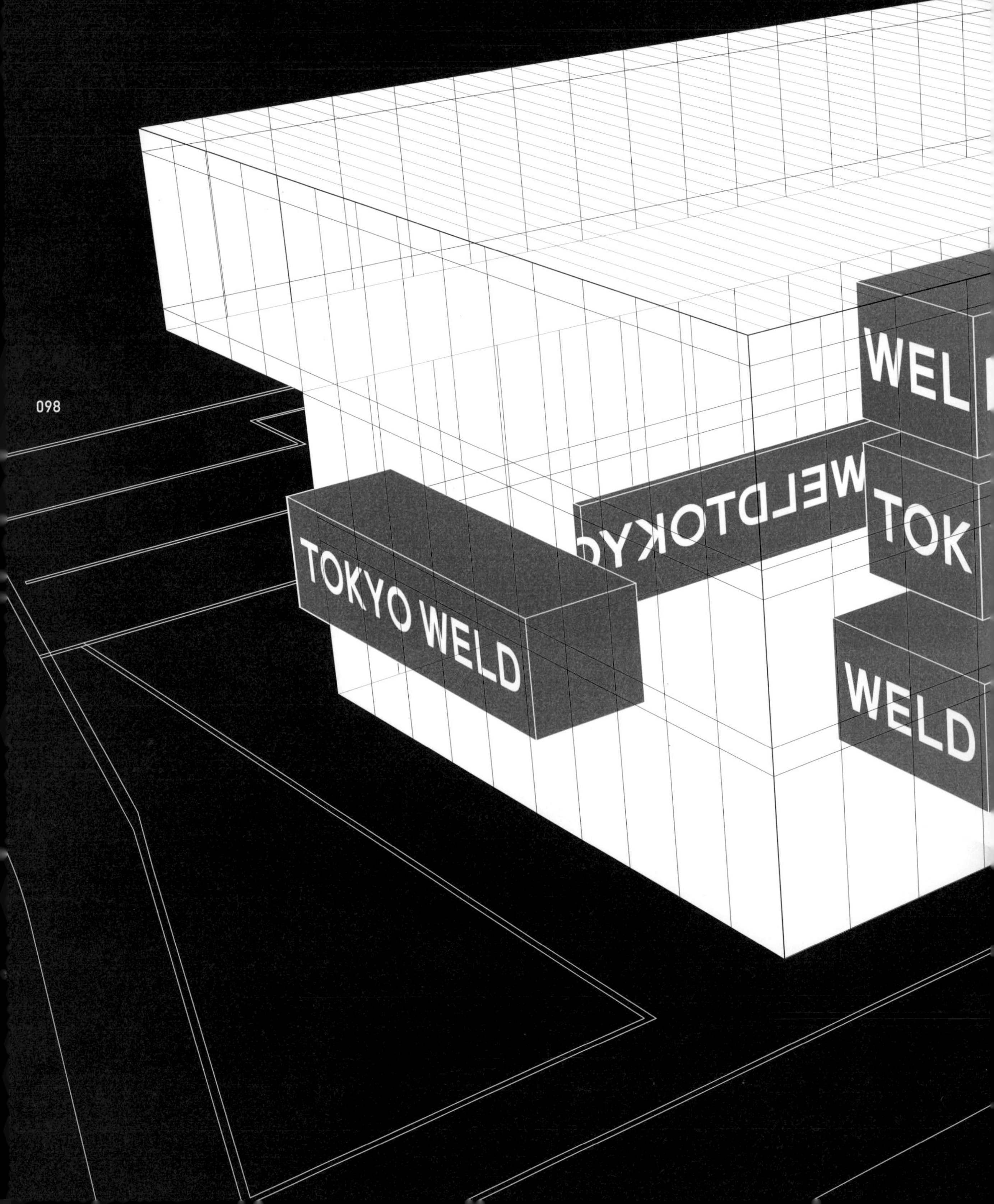

TOKYO WELD

WELDTOKYO

WEL

TOK

WELD

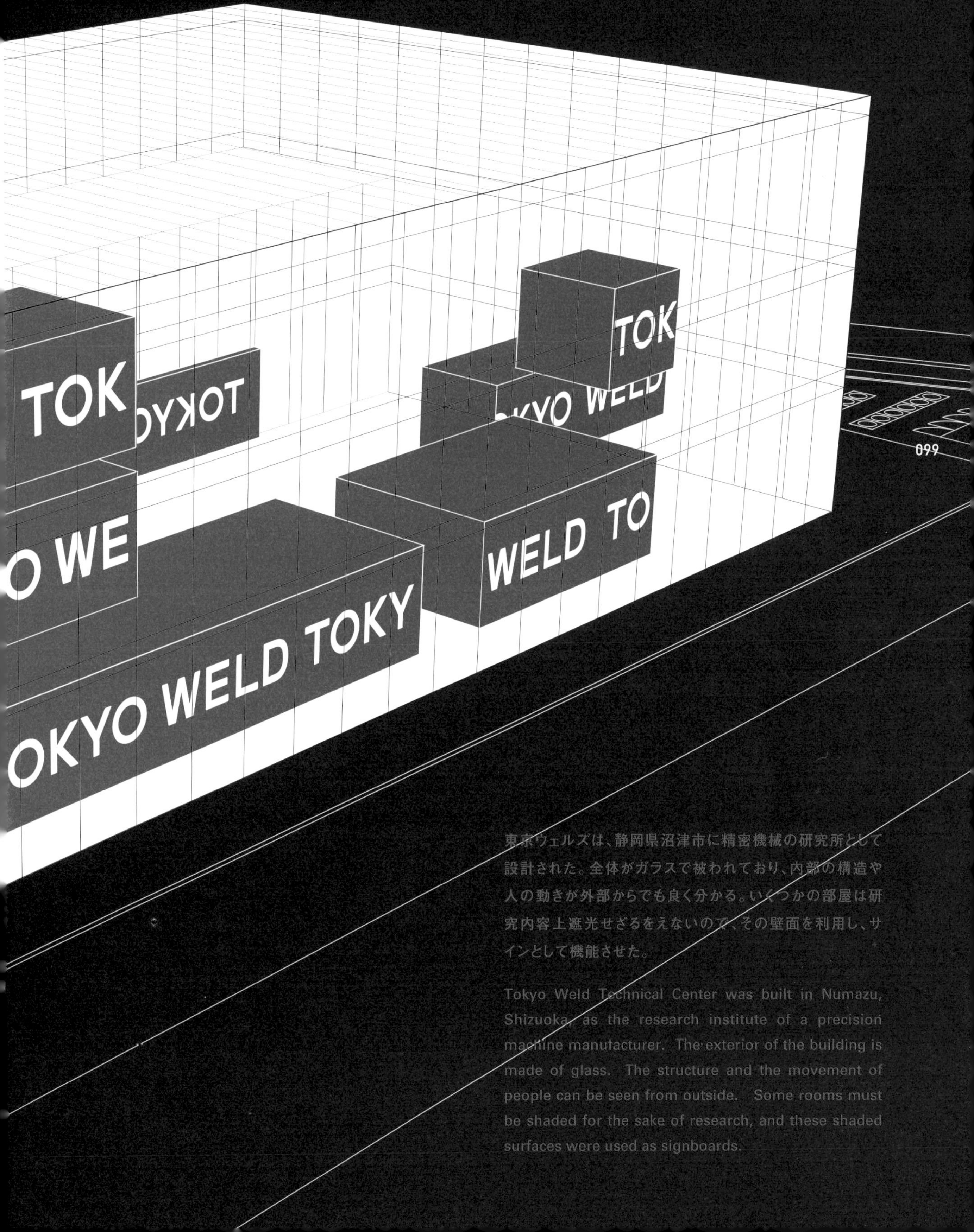

TOK

ТОКҮОТ

TOK

O WE

ОKYO WELD

WELD TO

OKYO WELD TOKY

東京ウェルズは、静岡県沼津市に精密機械の研究所として設計された。全体がガラスで被われており、内部の構造や人の動きが外部からでも良く分かる。いくつかの部屋は研究内容上遮光せざるをえないので、その壁面を利用し、サインとして機能させた。

Tokyo Weld Technical Center was built in Numazu, Shizuoka, as the research institute of a precision machine manufacturer. The exterior of the building is made of glass. The structure and the movement of people can be seen from outside. Some rooms must be shaded for the sake of research, and these shaded surfaces were used as signboards.

この研究所はコンピュータ用の電子チップの梱包システム等を開発しており、機械の設計や試作品のテスト、顧客へのプレゼンテーションをしている。そこで建物の内部の囲われた部屋の壁面に社名のロゴタイプを連続して表示する事にした。建物自体がサインになっているのだ。

This research institute is developing, among other things, package systems for electronic chips for computers. Researchers design machines, test products, and give presentations to their clients. The sign was designed by printing the logotype of the company continuously on the shades of shielded rooms. The building itself is functioning as a sign.

サインは全てカッティングシートを使用、ほとんどが通路の壁面やガラスの下地なので、費用と効果を考えると最適な選択だった。開かれたイメージの施設なのでサイン計画も、シンプルで分かりやすい事を最優先に考えた。

Stencil paper was used for the signs. This was an optimum choice considering cost effectiveness as the signs were applied to the walls of corridors and glass walls. As the building itself had an open image, the signs were also designed to be clear-cut and simple.

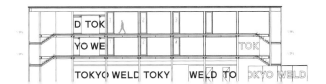

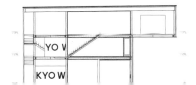

ガラスの建物に差し込まれているコンテナのような箱は機能が詰まったサインボックスである。都会のビル群に浮かび上がる塔屋ネオンのように、時間を追うごとに存在感を変化させている。

Container-like boxes inserted into the glass building are sign boxes acting for many purposes. Like neon signs on the roofs of buildings in large cities, they change their expressions as time passes.

入口の風除室を兼ねたガラスボックスは、両側を白いシートで貼り、ロゴタイプを透明に抜いた。日中は太陽の動きに合わせて影が風除室の床面に映り、時間を追うごとにシルエットを変えながら移動してゆく。

At the glass box at the entrance, acting also as a shelter from the wind, white sheets were pasted and the logotype was cut off. In the daytime, the shadow is reflected on the floor of the entrance hall, moving along the course of the sun.

夜になるとガラスボックスは大きな行灯になる。シンボルマークやロゴタイプが昼間とは反転し、光によって演出される。この研究所の外部にはサイン看板は無く、建物が大きなサイン塔になる。

In the evening, the glass box becomes a large lighthouse. The symbol marks and logotypes are presented in reverse from daytime. There is no signboard outside the premises of this building. The building itself is a large sign tower.

# 09
## 0901-0920

コモンテラス-B
Common Terrace-B

109

江東区東雲に建設中のこの集合住宅は、全体が1〜6街区に分かれ、それぞれの建築家チームで設計が行われている。1街区を設計している山本理顕さんとサインの相談をしている時に提案した郵便受けが、カラーストライプによるグラデーションだったことがきっかけとなり、各階を色分けして、各住戸の入口や外部に対し開口している部分にもカラーグラデーションを反映させることを考えた。

The large estate development project in Shinonome, Tokyo is divided into 6 districts, and a team of architects is assigned to each district. While discussing the sign system with architect Yamamoto Riken in charge of district 1, I proposed a mailbox with stripes in color gradation. This idea set the policy for using color gradation at the entrances to each building and other openings.

110

建物には中空の各所に穴が開いている。これはコモンテラスと呼ばれ、2層吹き抜けの共有スペースで、居住者が自由に使うことができる。このコモンテラスと共有の廊下を部分的に各階のカラーでストライプに塗る。このようなマンモス集合住宅では、各階同じ風景が連続するので、居住者に固有の色彩とパターンを持たせることで、誤認を避け、永く愛着を感じて欲しかった。

Square spaces are seen on the exterior wall of a building. These are two-story tall common spaces for residents to use freely. These common terraces and corridors are partially striped with a color specified to each floor. As similar scenes abound in the same estate, residents can easily identify their own buildings with the color and pattern specific to each building.

私は小学校から高校まで授業中に手を挙げたことがありません。極度のアガリ性のため、先生に指されただけでも頭が空白になり、冷や汗ものだったからです。でも、今になって思い返すと、頭が空白になるのには、アガリ性だけではない原因があったように思います。それは「自分の考えや意志を整理して相手に伝える」という技術が身についていなかったということです。

自分の意志を他人に説明すること（プレゼンテーション）は、デザインする事に不可欠な技術です。

思考の整理をして理論的に解りやすく伝えることができ、さらにそれが共感や感動を得られればもっと良いと思います。

昔から日本人には「語らずとも目を見れば解り合える」的な共通の美意識があり、寡黙は美徳という意識が今日でも残っています。一方、世代間の意識差やグローバル化が進む現実の社会では、単元的な発想や押しつけからは、多くの人々を説得させることはできません。プレゼンテーションはまず自分を、そして相手を理解することから始まります。その理解の上に立って、商品であれ作品であれ、すでにそのものが持ち、発している表現のエネルギーを、見せ方・伝え方のアイデアによって、浮かび上がらせなくてはならないのです。

展示構成やインスタレーションのように、対象物を最も効果的方法論で構築し提案することは、プレゼンテーションの技術がもっとも強く問われる舞台です。

空間という舞台にふさわしい表現の装置を組み、体感する人たちに、多くの感動と深い理解を与える新たな価値を生み出すことがプレゼンテーションの役割なのです。

112

Throughout my elementary to high school days, I never raised my hand to speak out. I was so nervous that when a teacher told me to give an answer, I would feel my head becoming empty, and break into a cold sweat. Looking back, it was not only because I was nervous that I felt my head to be empty, but I had not acquired the skill to convey what I wanted to say in an organized way.

This presentation skill is essential for designers. It is better if one can attract the listeners' interest and sympathy in addition to conveying one's ideas and intention.

We Japanese have long cherished a belief that "we can understand each other by looking at the other's eyes without any words." We still have an idea that "silence is a virtue." However, today, when generation gaps are widening, and globalization is progressing, we can no longer depend on the long-standing eye-contact communication.

For a presentation, we must begin with understanding ourselves, and the people to whom we will make the presentation. Then, we devise ways to show a product or a design work drawing on the expressive energy that the design work emits.

Exhibition composition and installations are the most demanding stages of presentation skills to show exhibits in the most effective method.

Designers feel a real zest in life when installing display devices best suited to a space, and placing exhibits in a way to strongly impress the viewers.

藤原新也 旅の軌跡展

企画：駒ヶ根高原美術館
展示ディレクション：廣村正彰
アート：藤原新也
デザイン：廣村正彰、水野佳史
施工：ヤマウラ、大沢POPレタリング、堀内カラー
クライアント：駒ヶ根高原美術館

Fujiwara Shinya "Travel Locus"

plan : Komagane Kogen Art Museum
exhibition direction : Hiromura Masaaki
art : Fujiwara Shinya
design : Hiromura Masaaki,
Mizuno Yoshifumi
construction : Yamaura,
Osawa Pop Lettering, Horiuchi Color
client : Komagane Kogen Art Museum

藤原新也 少年の港展

企画：パルコ
展示ディレクション：廣村正彰
アート：藤原新也
デザイン：廣村正彰、草谷隆文
展示協力：吉田淳
クライアント：パルコ

Fujiwara Shinya
"Syounen No Minato"

plan : Parco
exhibition direction : Hiromura Masaaki
art : Fujiwara Shinya
design : Hiromura Masaaki,
Kusagaya Takafumi
exhibition cooperation : Yoshida Jun
client : Parco

藤原新也 アメリカ

企画：パルコ
展示ディレクション：廣村正彰
アート：藤原新也
デザイン：廣村正彰、小島利之
展示協力：吉田淳
クライアント：パルコ

Fujiwara Shinya "America"

plan : Parco
exhibition direction : Hiromura Masaaki  113
art : Fujiwara Shinya
design : Hiromura Masaaki,
Kojima Toshiyuki
exhibition cooperation : Yoshida Jun
client : Parco

日本人とすまい 靴脱ぎ
Kutsu－Nugi

企画：Kutsu-Nugi企画委員会
アートディレクション：廣村正彰
展示デザイン：廣村正彰、小島利之
展示設計：岡本好司
マークイラストレーション：唐仁原教久
編集：住友和子
クライアント：オゾン

Japanese & Living Kutsu-Nugi

plan : Kutsu-Nugi Planning Committee
art direction : Hiromura Masaaki
exhibition design : Hiromura Masaaki,
Kojima Toshiyuki
exhibition plan : Okamoto Koji
mark illustration : Toujimbara Norihisa
editing : Sumitomo Kazuko
client : Ozone

1999 竹尾ペーパーショウ

アートディレクション：廣村正彰
デザイン：廣村正彰、小島利之、
草谷隆文、前田豊
会場構成：西沢立衛
照明：角館政英
コピー：日暮真三、高田美子
コーディネーション：高田事務所
編集：住友和子
写真：藤井保
展示協力：前田ジョン、
照沼太佳子（コーディネーション）
クライアント：竹尾

1999 Takeo Paper Show

art direction : Hiromura Masaaki
design : Hiromura Masaaki,
Kojima Toshiyuki, Kusagaya Takafumi,
Maeda Yutaka
hall construction : Nishizawa Ryue
lighting : Kakudate Masahide
copy : Higurashi Shinzo, Takata Yoshiko
coordination : Takata Office
editing : Sumitomo Kazuko
photograph : Fujii Tamotsu
exhibition cooperate : Maeda John,
Terunuma Takako(coordination)
client : Takeo

竹尾 見本帖本店

総合ディレクション：竹尾デザインコミッティ
（織咲誠、佐藤卓、原研哉、
平野敬子、廣村正彰）
デザイン：廣村正彰、木住野英彰
内装設計：西沢立衛
施工：清水建設
クライアント：竹尾

Takeo, Mihoncho Honten

direction : Takeo Design Community
(Orisaki Makoto, Satoh Taku,
Hara Kenya, Hirano Keiko,
Hiromura Masaaki)
design : Hiromura Masaaki,
Kishino Hideaki
interior architect : Nishizawa Ryue
construction : Shimizu
client : Takeo

そこに七ヶ月いて、アメリカという国はないんだなと思った

アメリカ　幻想を作るための、切磋琢磨はある。というひとつの

湾岸戦争　大統領選のお祭り騒ぎとか、とかね
だとか、
フットボールの馬鹿騒ぎ

そういったパフォーマンスが

アメリカという幻想を支えつづけている。

私は最終的に人間っていうのは

免疫不全で滅びると思ってる

114　TRAVEL LOCUS

本当の自分をさらけ出して

本当の人間関係ができる

の子供たちからは

奪い取られて

時間、年齢というものが

に突っ込まれてしまう

しまっている

ペンやカメラを持つということに対しては、

ぼくは逆にコンプレックスがある。

の上で

裸でスイカを逆さまに食っていた

あの肉体、

れはかなり存在しているわけで、

そのうしろにいる

カメラやペン

を寺つ自分という

できたのは死体だね。

六年くらい死体ばかり撮ってた時期があった。

いる人間より屍のほうに、思想がいっぱい詰まってようる気がしてね。

死生観──風土・環境の影響が大きい

無法地帯の混沌性

宗教の思想

アメリカにかかわる二十

ある家

いわゆる一「自然木」では

下意識の境準

湿合

旅の軌跡展は藤原新也氏がこれまでに発表してきた写真を中心に、氏の活動の全貌を知る展覧会である。「全東洋街道」に始まり、最近の「バリ」までの足跡をたどりながら、時代の流れを敏感に察知し、行く先々で焼き付けた映像を時間と場所の二つの軸で構成した。会場は長野県の駒ヶ根高原美術館、全館を使い立体的に組み立てた。

The exhibition "Travel Locus" was planned to show the photos and other activities of Fujiwara Shinya totally. His career is traced from the collection of "Roads of the Orient" and the most recent collection "Bali." The images printed by Fujiwara who is sensitive to changes of the world were displayed on the axes of time and places. Using the entire Komagane Kogen Art museum in Nagano prefecture, they were exhibited three-dimensionally.

砂に撒いた水のように
スッと消えていく。
だから日記をつけはじめたんだ。

皆
物語を求めてるんだね。
もうこの地球には結実のない一瞬のシーンしか残されていないのに……

人間が呼吸して何かをやろうとしている、
そのことすべてが尊いんだと思う。

それが悪であろうと善行であろうと、
生命が♂き動かしている人間の行動
という意味において、尊いんだと思う。

写真を撮る
ということは頭の中にある情報を消していく、
ある意味では子供みたいな視線を持たないといけない。
そしてはじめての事実としての物が見える。

俺は本音ほどいいかげんなものはないと思うんだけど、それはあくまで日本人の自然観なわけね、農耕民族の。
その自然観だけが残っちゃってるだけの話で、どんどん人工化して淫乱になっていく。
しって減退させると、あるがままだね、

いずれもっと過激な形で大きな社会的な事件が起きるような時には、
人間が、自らの存在を取り戻そうとする。
衝動的に予感がします。
もともと身体感のない

これはちょっと怖いですよ。
昨今の管理というのは、昔と違ってきわめて
社会全体が
不快なもの、危険なもの、異質なものをことごとく遠ざけ、
母性的。
子供の身体を囲っている。
過保護的に

118

人間は
やはり人類は自然から逃れようとしているんだなぁ
自然が好きと言われると、
自然から逃れようとしている
という実感があります。

メッセージ的言葉が人の心を変えるのか、逆にメッセージという形態に入っていけるのか、おそらく後者の方が人の心
自分の言葉、自分の生活を描いた時に入っていける時に、断念して、人の心
コミュニケーションの親密
今の子供は小学校に上がる頃から、
時間、年齢、競争社会
本当の人間関係ができるのが
奪い取られて
裸でスイカを逆さまに食っていた
あの肉体、
カメラやペン
コンプレックスをもった自分というのは
七ヶ月で、アメリカという国はないんだなと思った。
アメリカ幻想を作るための、
湾岸戦争 大統領選のお祭り騒ぎとか、フットボールの馬鹿騒ぎ
アメリカという幻想
私は最終的に人間っていうのは

免疫不全
「産業ハルマゲドン」「人口ハルマゲドン」もあり
『言葉』
「免疫不全ハルマゲドン」
で滅びると思ってる。

言葉や芸術こそが
それの代用として
人間の心を育む
言葉というのは予定
たとえば
人間は犬に食われるほど自由だ
この日本社会の中の
管理の中で
管理もまた言葉を生むのです。

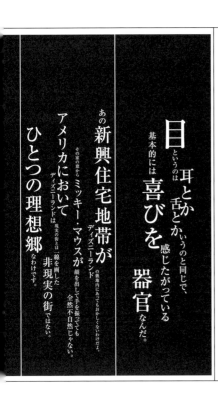

タイ

これはイスタンブールから中近東を通ってアジアへと動いたわけだけど、結局、殺伐とした空気が残る

むしろ物

物には人間の心がこもる

確かに

その匂いは確かに日本から流れてくる

今度はもう少し向こうから来ているような気がしたのね

アメリカなんです。

誕生日 命日

かつての家族については、

アメリカでは ハッピー・バースデー、って。

幸福

アメリカ化してるのね。

しかし最近の

命日がないのね。誕生日すごく祝うわけ。

二十世紀の

虚構文明の旅

をたどりよせいく。やがてアメリカに行き着く。

自分の生物としての存在を抹消していかれる。

そういうものの発祥している

エーテルみたいな

戒律、

旅の場所

というのは、ある場所から場所へ移動している最中に、

自分の中にイメージされるもうひとつの

架空の場所

でもあるわけです。

移動そのものの発想の中に

場所があるのではないかと思う。

目

というのは耳とか舌とかいうのと同じで、基本的には

喜びを

感じたがっている

器官なんだ。

あの

新興住宅地帯が

その家の裏からミッキー・マウスが顔を出して手を振っても全然不自然じゃない。

アメリカにおいて

ディズニーランドは現実の街と一線を画した

ひとつの理想郷

なわけです。非現実の街ではない。

ヒマラヤは……、そこにある菩提樹も、ガンジス川も……

ヒンドゥー教は世界宗教

だから

僕の旅は自分の

場所さがし

自分の場所がない。

門司港でやってた旅館が区画整理で壊された。

神戸へと

ボランティアで熱狂的に

私には崩壊というユートピアへ向かって走っていく若者たちの姿は、

迷える羊

のように見えた。

自然は、

自然は、モラルや

リアリティを保つ。

アメリカ人は

根ついてない。

こいつらは根っこが

資本主義

共産主義

コンプレックス

旅行者のままだ。

習慣、宗教

目の前の現実が

アジアにある

神という

誇大妄想

に逃げる。

神様を見るほうが楽なわけです。もう終わりですよ。

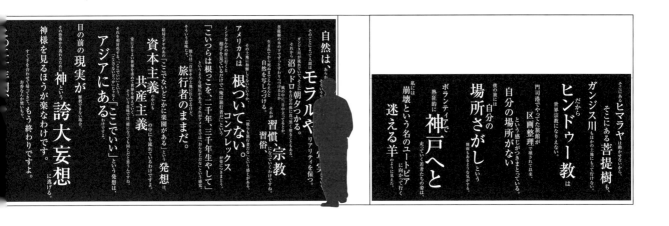

氏の表現手法は写真に限定されていない。文章も大きな魅力でファンが多い。会場には部屋と部屋を結ぶ通路があり、意識がそこで途切れてしまう。そこで強く印象的な言葉を選んでもらい、グラフィカルに構成して天井から瀧のように流した。この「言葉の瀧」が幻想的な各部屋を結ぶ接続詞として全体の大きな流れを作った。

Fujiwara's means of expression are not limited to photography. His essays are also attractive. In an exhibition, viewers' perceptions of the exhibition are interrupted while they move from one room to another. Therefore, we asked him to choose impressive phrases from among his essays, which we then printed graphically on cloths. We then hung the printed cloths like curtains on the walls of the corridors from the ceiling. These "phrase falls" served as connectors between exhibit rooms.

各部屋にはタイトルが、黒く大きな表札のように立っている。それぞれの部屋は作品の密度が濃く、全体を一気に通して観るには体力がいる。入口で気持ちの準備をして次の世界へ突入する必要がある。作品は印画紙だけでなく、大型のデジタルプリントをロールのまま吹き抜けの天井から垂らしたり、水面の写真を床の上に水平に設置したり、なるべく非現実的でダイナミックな演出をした。

The exhibited works were highly contemplative, and viewers need mental strength to appreciate the pieces. Therefore, exhibit titles were printed on large black cloths and shown at the entrance to help the viewers to be prepared before entering a room. Photos were shown not only by photo panels but also as large digital prints in a roll displayed from the ceiling of the two-story high room. The photos of water surface were placed right on the floor. Thus, we attempted to show his photos in a dynamic manner.

## 「破壊」のススメ

## 藤原新也 × 廣村正彰

時間と距離と音の演出

廣村：藤原さんに初めてお会いしたのは、『アメリカ』展より12〜3年前、僕が田中一光先生のところに所属していた時、事務所にいらしたんですよ。見たこともないような原風景を捉える写真が多かったという印象があります。広告写真がどんどんクローズアップされていた当時においては、異質な写真で、人間の悩みをドロドロと出しているのに、すごくきれいで衝撃的でした。その後、僕が独立したあと、1990年にパルコで開催された写真集『アメリカ』の展覧会をお手伝いさせていただいたのが始まりだった。

藤原：なぜあのとき廣村君と仕事することになったのか、その経緯は今は覚えていないんですが。

廣村：僕もフリーになった直後で、パルコの人が紹介してくれたんです。展覧会のグラフィックを見せにお伺いした時に、「ついでに会場構成を一緒にやらないか」と誘ってもらった。会場構成に携わったのは初めてだったし、すごく気合いが入ってしまって。「何をやってもいいよ」とパルコ側も言うので、工事現場で使うパイプで構成して、床にゴムシートを貼って…、

藤原：床にゴムを敷きつめてね。会場がデパートの催事場だから、アプローチがなく、ひょいと覗いたら会場が全部見えてしまうようなスペースなのが嫌で、それでお宮参りの参道のようなものをつくろうということになったんですね。工事現場で使う鉄板を太鼓橋のように渡して起伏をつけて、一度上がって、横を回って下りるようにした。

廣村：店舗がひしめく現実的な空間から、作品に出会う会場の間には時間と距離が必要だということが、まず最初に藤原さんから教わったことでした。現実からのタイムラグを会場構成で演出すること、そのためにアプローチの役割がかなり大きいということを考えさせられました。その後、93年の『少年の港展』でも、真白な壁に囲まれた狭い通路を抜けて会場に入るという演出をしました。

藤原：それにしても『アメリカ』の時は、床のゴムの匂いが効いていた。人工的なもののように見えながら植物が原料だという、ある種の妙な感覚もあって、結果的にひとつの雰囲気づくりになりましたね。

廣村：近所の店舗からクレームがつくほどすごい臭いでしたね。

藤原：それから鉄の橋桁を渡る時の、「ゴンゴンゴン」という足音がものすごく印象的だった。BGMはあまり好きではないけれど、あの会場には人工的な足音が『アメリカ』の風景と妙にマッチしていた。

## "Destruction" for Building Something New

## Fujiwara Sinya ✕ Hiromura Masaaki

Creating the Senses of Time, Distance and Sound

Hiromura: I first met you more than 20 years ago, when I saw your photos. These photos were of natural scenes of people's life expressing human agony, but I thought they were beautiful.  I remember I had a strong impression, rather, shocking impression, from your photos.  Later, when you had the exhibition "America" at Parco in Tokyo, I helped with the making of the exhibition hall.  When I called on you to show my graphics for your exhibition, you told me "How about constructing the exhibition hall together?"  As it was my first assignment to design an exhibition hall, I was a little over-spirited.  Parco's people told me "Do as you like," so I used pipes used at construction sites for the structure, and pasted rubber sheets on the floor.

Fujiwara: The exhibition hall was a multipurpose room in a department store, and when you opened the door, you could see the entire hall at sight. I did not like that, so we decided to create an approach. Then we brought an iron sheet that is used for a construction site and bent it like an arched bridge to lead the visitors to go up, turn once and go down to the floor.

Hiromura: Time and a distance are necessary to lead the audience from the world of reality to an encounter with art works.  This is the first thing that I learned through working with you.  You made me realize that we need to create a time lag from the real world by designing an exhibition hall, and that an approach plays an important role for that purpose.  When I worked for another exhibition of yours, "Syounen no minato (Harbor in Boyhood Memories) in 1993, I designed a narrow approach of white walls to the exhibition hall.

Fujiwara: I remember that the smell of the rubber sheets on the floor were effective for the "America."  Rubber looks like man-made chemical products, but in fact, it is made from a plant.  With this strange feeling, the rubber sheets successfully helped create an appropriate atmosphere for the exhibition.

Hiromura: The smell was so strong that shops nearby complained about it.

Fujiwara: And the sound that the iron bridge made when people walked over it was also impressive.  In that hall, those artificial sounds fitted well to the scenes of "America."

## 積み上げながら、壊しながら

廣村：藤原さんの写真は、それまで原風景のようなものが多かったのが、『アメリカ』では
人工的なものが大きなテーマになっていましたね。アメリカという国は風景やモノだけで
なく、人間そのものも移民という意味では「原」ではない。そうしたものが広い大地の上
に浮いているようなイメージがあった。それをうまく表現したかった。そんなことを考えなが
ら、藤原さんの提案を僕が形にしていったということだと思います。勉強させてもらいました。

藤原：お互いのキャッチボールのなかででき上がっていくのがいちばん面白いですよね。

廣村：面白いのは、藤原さんは突然に、それまで積み上げてきたもの全部を崩して
しまうことがあること。それはかなりの勇気がいると思います。つくり上げてきた本人が
いちばん壊したくないはずなのに、突然冷静に壊してしまう。アーティストは自分の
世界に入り込んで、自分の世界を客観的に見ない人が多いように感じるのですが、
藤原さんの場合は、ちょっと引きながら常に客観的に自分の世界を見て、なにか違う
かもしれないと思うとバラッと崩してしまって、また別のものを創るということがある。

126　藤原：作品との距離というのは、キャッチボールをしている相手との距離でもある
と思っているんです。だから、冷たく距離を保ちながら見ることができて、煮詰まり過ぎ
ているということもわかる。それに誰かと一緒にやる時には、最初は何も言わない
ようにしているんです。初めからコミュニケーションを密にしてしまうと、こちらの意向
を予め汲み取ったものしか出てこないですね。それじゃつまらない。廣村君は何を
考えるだろう、というところに興味があるわけだから。

## 空間だからこその表現を

廣村：藤原さんと付き合っていて思ったのは、写真家であるというより表現者だと
いうことなんです。写真はひとつの表現手法であって、土台はもっと広いんです。たと
えば文章の力もものすごく強い。『東京漂流』の時から読んでいますが、藤原さんの
言葉は、文章というよりキャッチフレーズが集まってできているように思えます。それを
そのまま展示に流れ込ませる方法がないかと考えたのが『旅の軌跡展』のアプロー
チでした。階段を昇って各展覧会場に入るまでのプロセスに、天井から文字をダーッ
と垂らした。藤原さんの表現の力は文字だけを読んでいてもグイグイと迫ってくるも
のがある。それだけに写真を見る序章としては、かなりドラマチックな導入となる。

藤原：廣村君の文字のあつかいにはいつも感心してるんです。最近の人は基礎から
やっていないから文字をあつかわせるとヨレヨレでしょ。その意味ではあの会場では
文字構成によって全体がビシッとしまりました。

廣村：藤原さんの作品というのは、展覧会で実際に目の当たりにして初めてわかることが
すごく多いと思います。本ではわからない、その場だからこそ体験できることを空間の演出

Building up and Demolishing

Hiromura: Many of your photos before "America" were about natural scenes of places and people's life. But in "America," "being artificial" was one of the main motifs. In a sense, the USA is not "natural" not only in its townscapes but also as a country comprising immigrants from different places. I had an image that non-natural things were floating on the huge land, and I wanted to give an expression to that image. You gave me inspiration and I gave a shape to your idea.

Fujiwara: It is most interesting to see that something can be built up by people throwing and catching a ball each other.

Hiromura: What surprised me was that you sometimes demolish what you had built up all of a sudden. You have to be very courageous to do so. A creator must be the last person to destroy what one has worked on. But you suddenly destroy quite coolly what you have made. I often feel that artists are the kind of people who are engrossed in their own worlds and who do not see their worlds objectively. You keep a few steps away from the world of your own art, and look at it objectively. And if you find something that you feel unfit to your idea, you destroy a work on progress and start making a new one from the beginning.

Fujiwara: The distance between my work and myself is like the distance between two persons playing catch. By looking at my work from a distance, I can find if the work is overdone. When I work with someone, I do not give directions or instructions at the beginning. If I explain what I want in detail, the partner will grasp my idea and try to propose designs that suit that without giving his own. It is not interesting. My interest in working in partnership with someone lies in seeing what the partner will think.

Expressions that only suit a space

Hiromura: I see that you are more than just a photographer. Photographing is one of the tools of expression for you. You write with a strong style. I have read your books since Tokyo Hyoryu (Drifting in Tokyo). Every time I read your book, I feel that the book consists of catchphrases rather than sentences and I have been thinking how I could use these phrases at your exhibitions. So I applied this idea to make an approach to each exhibition room at the "Travel Locus" exhibition. I hung cloths on which phrases are written from the ceiling. Just by reading these phrases, your versatility in expression comes pressingly into the readers' minds. So, these phrases served as dramatic introductions to your photographs.

Fujiwara: I am always amazed with the way you deal with letters. Indeed, the use of letters gave a tense sensation to that exhibition.

Hiromura: There are lots of discoveries to be made in your photos when I see them closely at an exhibition, which I won't find by looking at them printed in a book. It

によって実現しなければならない。装飾的に華美にすることではなく、内面を出すためにどうするのか。それを毎回突きつけられながら仕事をするところが、他の展覧会とは全然違う。

藤原：昔は、写真展という形には全然興味がなかった。雑誌に載った写真を壁にかけても、どうなるものでもないし、どういうメディアであっても変わらないと思っていた。それが初めて写真展をやることになった時、どうせ空間に置くなら、何か意味がないと面白くないんじゃないかと考えたんです。どういう見せ方をするかということが、写真展でいちばん大切なことだと思った。空間構成は本当はまったく違った媒体なのだから、エディトリアルの延長線上で写真展をやっても何の意味もない。


波風のない仕事はつまらない


**廣村：藤原さんと仕事をするまで、僕には芸術作品はある種不変なものだという認識があったんです。そうではないとわかりました。**

藤原：絵でも写真でも芸術指向があるけれど好きじゃない。後生大事に壁に飾って、芸術性がどうだこうだという雰囲気はすごく嫌いなんです。何であろうと僕は「遊び」だと思っている。人生なんてたいしたことはない、絵だろうが写真だろうが、しょせんは遊びじゃないかというようなものがある。だから、写真展によって空間で作品を見て、それによって人が抱く価値観が変わっても少しも構わない。廣村君と相性がいいのは、そのせいだと思う。僕は無茶苦茶だけれど、廣村君は基本がしっかりしていて、そこから積み上げて仕事をしている数少ない人ですからね。僕自身が作家としてのセオリーを崩しているわけだから、素人に毛のはえたような無茶苦茶なことをするデザイナーと組んでも、ちっとも面白くない。廣村君のように基本の積み重ねがある人と、投げ合いをして壊していく面白さが好きだしね。形が違うから上手くいっているんだと思う。

**廣村：僕はマゾヒスティックなところがあるのか、壊されることが嫌いじゃないんです。逆に、壊してくれないですんなりオーケーを出されると「本当にこれでいいの?」と困ってしまう時がある。**

藤原：途中で紆余曲折がなかったものや、「この野郎」と感情的になることなくすんなりいった作品というのは、大概あまりよくない。感情的になったり、ぶつかったりしながら生み出されたもののほうが高まりがあるし、多少そういうやりとりがないとやっていても面白くない。それに、そうしてやり合えるということは、相手に対しても自分に対しても誠実なことですよ。

**廣村：確かに、それぞれが役割分担の中でのみ仕事をして、お互いを容認だけしているという姿勢は、ある種無責任だとも思います。お互いに介入していかないと、本当に100パーセント納得できるものになるわけがない。**

藤原：昨今は子どもの時から「波風を立たさないように」と教育されてくるけれど、気持ちよく終わらせることだけ考えて仕事をするのは無責任だと思う。それは「何も言わない」ということですからね。

means that I must create an environment in the exhibition hall to help the viewers find these points. How can I design the hall and arrange your photos in order to draw out the implications hidden inside? I work with such a challenge thrust before me.

Fujiwara: I was not interested in photo exhibitions at the beginning. I thought it would be nonsense to hang photos on the wall to show what had been already published in magazines. When it was decided that my first photo exhibition would be held, I thought I should express some of the significance of this change when I hung my photos in a space. I realized that how to show the photos to the audience is the most important issue for a photo exhibition. An exhibition space is completely different from editing pages in a magazine, so it would be meaningless to display photos in a hall as if it was merely an extension of editorial design.

Working without conflict is not interesting.

Fujiwara: The reason that both of us get along with each other well is that we are different. I do things as I like. But you are one of a few designers who studied basics firmly, and have accumulated experiences. Since I am breaking the theory as a creator, if I work with a designer who has a similar style like myself, then the result would be miserable. I like to exchange ideas with someone like you who has acquired basic skills and to destroy what has been built up.

Hiromura: For myself, I don't have any ill feeling towards you when you destroy what I have made. Rather, I would feel uneasy if you commented, "It's good, OK," at first sight. Sometimes I feel puzzled and wonder "Is that really alright?"

Fujiwara: Works created without any turns and twists in the process, or works made smoothly without feeling emotional opposition from someone working with me often end up being merely mediocre. Works made after becoming emotional or having conflicts with someone often turn out to be better. Without an exchange of views, the process of creation is not interesting. To communicate well with a partner means that both of us can be honest to ourselves and our partners.

Hiromura: Certainly, the style that each person employs within one's range of responsibility and admits other's works mutually, may be amicable but irresponsible in a sense. Unless there is an exchange of views among those involved in one work with different responsibilities, the whole creation will not become a satisfactory one.

Fujiwara: These days, children are taught from their early childhood that they should not quarrel with others. If you are concerned only about completing one work without having ill feelings to anyone, you are not performing your responsibility fully for the work. It will mean that you will keep your mouth shut.

## 「けものみち」はつくらない

廣村：藤原さんとはいつも一緒に仕事をしているわけではないし、時には5年くらい間隔があって、また久しぶりに会ったりしていますよね。そうするとかえって距離感がわかったりして、いっぱい話を聞きたくなる。失礼な言い方ですけれど、やはり人間・藤原が面白いからなんだと思います。僕が思うに、「藤原新也」とは、常に裏切り続けているということ。そこに魅かれる。

藤原：表現者の基本ですよ。たとえば、僕の場合は常に読者がいる。お互いに気持ち良さのなかで同時進行している時に、ある時突然、パーンと違うところに行ってしまう。その「裏切り」がいいんです。それは自分をも裏切ることですから、結構しんどい。同じことをガンコに続けるというのは一見きついようで楽なことなんですよ。

廣村：不思議な人だと言うしかない。でもそれがいいと思う。

藤原：廣村君は、自分の文体をどこかでぶち壊したいという欲求はありますか。

廣村：あります。こうした空間の仕事というのは、日頃グラフィックデザインをやっているのとは別の切り口だと思っていますし、デザイナーとしての自分の表現方法の可能性のひとつだと考えています。

藤原：廣村君も、自分の壊す楽しみが基本的にある人なんですよ。いろんな積み木をたくさん積み重ねているから、今からどんどん壊す作業のなかで仕事をしてほしいですね。だいたい人間というのは非常に保守的なものだからね。動物というものはみんなそうですよ。野生の動物はいっぺん歩いた道を必ず歩くから、森や山には獣道（けものみち）ができる。人間も家から駅までの道順はおおよそ決まっている。だけど、たまには動物としての基本をはずしたいじゃないですか。時にはぜんぜん違う道を通りたいとか、たまには違う店で食べてみようとか、考えたい。そこに、日常に潜む保守性を壊していく楽しみがある。僕らは川原乞食のようなもので、ある種の芸人です。そういう人たちが毎日同じルートを通るような生活をしていたら、見る側は面白くない。

廣村：予測できるということは、つまらない。デザインも予測できるところで納めてもつまらないということですね。

藤原新也　写真家、作家
1944年福岡県生まれ。東京芸術大学油画科中退。アジア放浪の旅に出て、『印度放浪』、『西蔵放浪』（ともに朝日新聞社刊）等を著し、以後時代を撮り、時代を語る。78年『西蔵放浪』『逍遥游記』（ともに朝日新聞社刊）『七彩夢幻』（パルコ出版）で木村伊兵衛写真賞を、82年『全東洋街道』（集英社刊）で毎日芸術賞を受賞。主な著書に『東京漂流』、『メメント・モリ』、『アメリカ』（以上情報センター出版局刊）、『ショットガンと女』（集英社インターナショナル刊）、『空から恥が降る』（文藝春秋刊）。写真集に『少年の港』（扶桑社刊）、『千年少女』（スイッチ・コーポレーション刊）、『俗界富士』、『バリの雫』、『鉄輪』（以上新潮社刊）がある。

We do not make an animal trail.

Hiromura: We work together from time to time. Sometimes, we do not see each other for five years or so. When there is such a lapse of time, I cannot help wanting to listen to your stories, because I find that your personality is interesting and attractive. I feel that "Fujiwara Shinya" is a person who continuously outwits me, and I am attracted to you for this.

Fujiwara: It is my basic attitude. I have readers, and while the readers and myself are going together in comfort, I suddenly go to another place. This unexpected departure is good. This means that I have to change the direction of my work, which is quite hard to do. To keep on doing the same thing may appear to be hard, but in fact, it is much easier.

Hiromura: I have no other words to describe you than to say that "you are a person of wonder," which is the reason that I am interested in you.

Fujiwara: Do you have a desire to destroy your own style somehow?

Hiromura: Yes. Working for a space is one approach to breaking my ordinary work style as a graphic designer. It expands the means of my expression as a creator.

Fujiwara: You basically find pleasure in destroying your own work style. You have piled up many experiences like building bricks. So, I want you to create your future works while destroying your style positively. Humans are basically conservative in nature, just as all other animals. Wild animals walk the paths that they walked before, so animal trails are made in the mountains and forests. Most people follow the same route to go to nearby stations. But sometimes, you may feel like taking a different route, or eating at a different restaurant, or doing something that is different from your daily habits. You will find it agreeable to destroy the conservatism that is embedded in daily life. We are entertainers of a sort, so if we live a life by which we continue taking the same route every day, the audience will be tired of looking at our performances.

Hiromura: The audience will not be interested in what they can predict to occur. It is true with design. Predictable designs are mediocre.

Fujiwara Shinya, photographer · writer

Born in Fukuoka in 1944. Left Tokyo National University of Fine Arts and Music (oil painting). Traveled in Asia and published *Indo Horo* (Traveling in India) and *Tibet Horo* (Traveling in Tibet) (Both Asashi Shimbun-sha), after which he photographed and wrote essays and non-fictions on happenings in society. In 1978, he won Kimura Ihei Photography Award for *Tibet Horo and Syoyo Yuki* (Strolling Journal in East Asia) (both Asahi Shimbun-sha) and *Shichisai Mugen* (Seven Colored World of Dreams) (Parco). In 1982, he received the Mainichi Art Award for *Zen Toyo Kaido* (All Oriental Routes) (Shueisha). His other major publications include *Tokyo Hyoryu* (Drifting in Tokyo), *Memento Mori, America* (The above three, Joho Center Publishing), *Shotgun to Onna* (Shotgun and Women) (Shueisha International), *Sora kara Haji ga Furu* (Shame is falling down from the sky.) (Bungeishunju), *Syounen no Minato* (Harbor in Boyhood Memories) (Fuso Publishing), *Sennen Syojo* (Girls Living for Thousand Years)(Switch Corporation), *Zokukai Fuji* (Mt. Fuji in the Secular World), *Bali no Shizuku* (Drops in Bali), and *Kannawa* (Iron Rope) (The above three, Shinchosha).

SYOUNEN NO MINATO

「少年の港」展は、藤原氏の故郷である門司を撮り下ろし　133
た写真展である。氏と同時に観客も意識のタイムスリップ
をしてもらう為に、白くて長い導入路を通過するようにした。
そこを抜けると薄暗い会場に、記憶の断片が浮かび上がる。
もちろん現代の写真だがインスタレーションにより、作家と
シンクロする感覚が得られればと考えた。

The "SYOUNEN NO MINATO" (Harbor in Boyhood
Memories) exhibition showed the photos of Moji port,
his hometown, that he had taken for the exhibition. In
order to help Fujiwara and the audience feel like they
were traveling back to childhood, a long white
approach was prepared. Passing through it, fragments
of childhood memories appeared to be floating in the
dim room. The port scenes in the photos are
contemporary ones, but we hoped that the viewers
would share synchronic feelings with Fujiwara from the
image they feel from the retrospective installations.

「アメリカ」展は、藤原氏との初めての仕事だった。写真を眺めていると表面的に虚飾な部分と、限り無く空虚なアメリカの現実を感じた。そこで展示は建築現場で使うポールを組み立て、友人に染めてもらった綿布で廻りを被い、床に黒いゴムシートを敷いて構成した。しかしファッションビルの中なので、周りのテナントから、臭いと音のクレームが続出、マイッタ。

Fujiwara's "America" exhibition was the first exhibition that I worked on for Fujiwara. While looking at his photos, I felt ostentatious parts and endless emptiness in the realities of America. To exhibit these photos, I decided to assemble poles that are used at construction sites. I asked one of my friends to dye cotton fabric to wrap around the poles. On the floor, black rubber sheets were laid. As the exhibition was held in a fashionable building, we had to apologize to the tenants who complained about noise and smell.

新宿のリビングデザインセンターOZONEで開催された「く
つぬぎ」は、住いと日本人をテーマに毎年行われる企画展
の第一回目である。履物を脱いで家に入るという行為は、
単にアジアの風土性に起因する習慣という事だけでなく、
住いが神聖なエリアである事の証しでもある。土間から板
間へ、それから畳へとそれぞれ結界を越え、聖域に入る為
に人は履物を脱ぐ。

The "Kutsu-Nugi" exhibition at the Living Design Center
Ozone Hall was the first exhibition under the theme of
Japanese & Living. Taking off footwear to enter a
house is a habit originating in the climate in Asia. It
suggests that a house is a holy place. From an earth
floor part to wooden floor rooms and further to tatami-
matted rooms, people take off their footwear to pass
through thresholds and proceed to the sacred area.

展示は全て床面で構成し、それを見る為に観客には全員靴を脱いでもらった。藁や竹など昔は素足に感じた素材を実際に体感しながら、会場を自由に廻り、疲れたらゴロンと横になれるように設えた。またイラストレーターの唐仁原さんにシンボルになる絵を描いてもらい、ポスターや本の表紙、会場の中にも貼って、ヴィジュアルの統一をした。

We placed all the exhibits on the floor. We asked all visitors to take off their shoes. Straws and bamboos were abundantly used to allow the visitors to feel them with their barefoot. A space for rest was also prepared for them to lie down. I asked illustrator Toujimbara to design a symbol and used for posters and a book cover.

Kutsu-Nugi

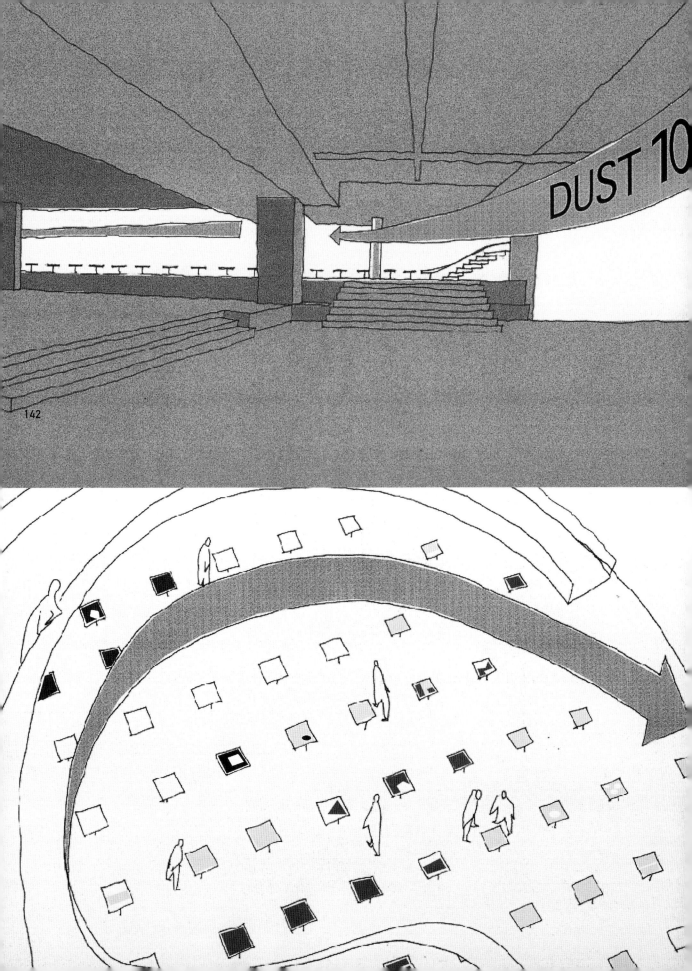

DUST 10

竹尾ペーパーショウは、学生やデザイナー、印刷業の方々に紙を広く知ってもらう事を目的に、毎年青山のスパイラルで開催されている。99年度の担当に指名され、テーマを「紙の十字架」に決めた。会場構成などは建築家の西沢立衛さんとコラボレーションして進めた。このページは西沢氏の初期のプランで、矢印が入口から1階の展示をぐるっと廻り、3階の会場までつながる考え方で、誘導サインとしての役割も果たしている。

The Takeo Paper Show is held every year in Tokyo with the purpose of having paper better known to design students, designers and printing company workers. The theme for the 1999 show was decided to be the "Cross of Paper." I worked with architect Nishizawa Ryue to compose the exhibition hall. The plan in this page was his early plan. From the entrance, the arrow went around the exhibits on the 1st floor and continued to the hall on the 3rd floor. It also served as a guide sign.

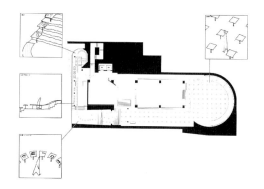

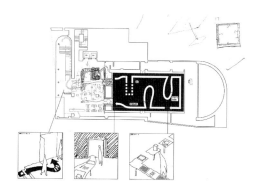

紙の展示で一番困るのは、紙自体よりも加工されたものが
評価の対象になってしまうことで、凝った印刷や複雑なパッ
ケージなどを展示することが今までは多かった。しかし今回
はデザインする行為より、紙が本来持っている魅力を伝え
たくて、同じ紙でもパターンを変えることで、まったく質感の
違う紙になることを体感してもらったり、100色以上のカラ
ーバリエーションを持つ紙を、色味と明度のチャートに分け、
使用量による高低差をつけて立体的に展示した。種類にも
驚くが、日本は世界で有数の紙開発国であることも、改めて
実感した。

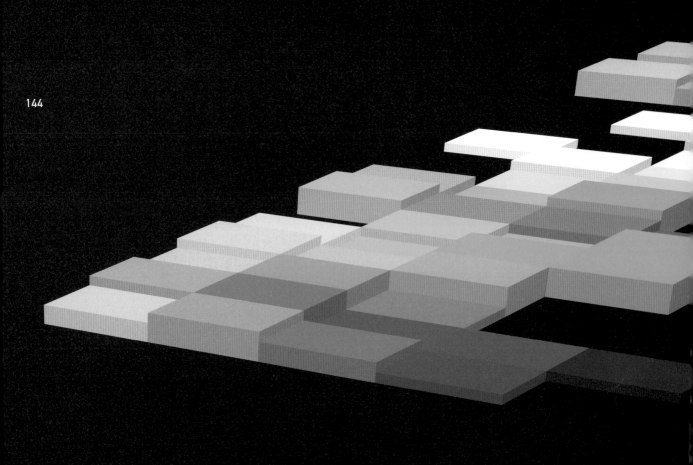

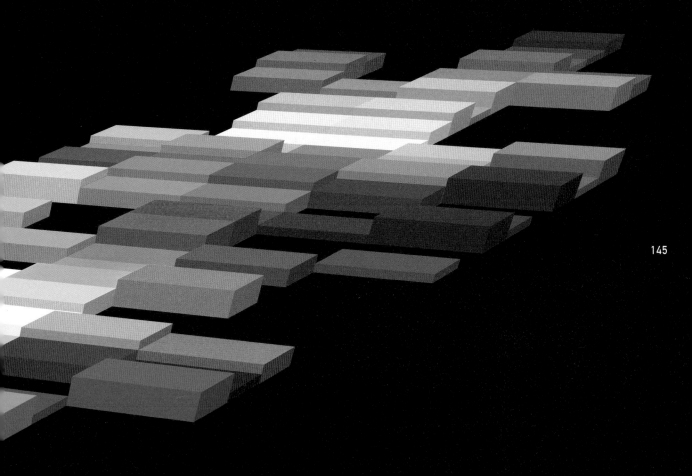

The greatest setback of a paper exhibition is that visitors tend to appreciate processed things rather than paper exhibits themselves. In the past exhibitions, elaborate prints and complicated packages have been exhibited. In this 1999 show, we tried to show the charm of various kinds of paper. We show the same paper in different patterns to help viewers to realize different textures created from the same paper. We also arranged one kind of paper available in more than 100 colors grouping by hues and brightness, and laid them in different heights according to their respective volume of sales. There are amazingly many varieties of paper, and I realized that Japan is a leading country in developing paper products.

146 「紙の十字架」とは、ここ数年環境に対する問題意識が高まり、その最大のターゲットが木材を原料とする紙に集中していて、実際には誤解されている部分も多いのだが、紙が背負っている問題と、今後の可能性をここでハッキリさせておくべきだと、コピーライターの日暮真三さんにタイトルを付けてもらった。1階では100人のクリエイターにゴミをテーマに出品してもらい、60cm角のテーブルに展示する「DUST100」を。1階から3階の階段にはテーブルが連続して並び、紙に関わる事を記述。3階のホールでは大きなテーブルに、環境や新製品、デジタルなどテーマごとに分けて展示。デジタル対応紙では、前田ジョンさんにインタラクティブなソフトを作っていただいた。

For the past several years, environmental concerns have mounted among the public, and paper made from timber has been the target of criticism. Although this criticism is caused largely from misunderstanding, I thought that we should clearly present the problems that paper manufacturing is shouldered with and the potentiality it has. Higurashi Shinzo, copywriter, gave a title of "the Cross of Paper" to this exhibition. The "DUST 100" on the first floor exhibited works by 100 creators with trash as the theme, each on a 60-sq. cm.- table. A table was placed on each step of the staircase from 1st to 3rd floors to give explanations about paper. On the large table in the hall on the 3rd floor, exhibits were grouped under different captions such as the Environment, New Products, Digital Technology. To show paper used to print digitized data, Maeda John created an interactive software program.

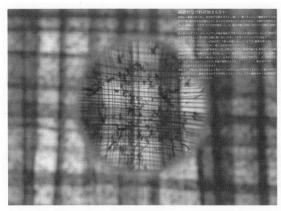

展示会のプロモーションと会場で渡す冊子の撮影を藤井
保さんにお願いした。紙をつくる為に必要な、木と水のイメ
ージとして森と海を、そこに紙の象徴として白い本の塔を建
てて、テーマをヴィジュアル化したポスターを制作した。（P150、
151参照）冊子は紙と環境を考える為に、古代の紙や野菜
などの繊維を拡大して、紙の成り立ちを考えたり、焼却や漂

白を視覚化して環境にどのような影響を及ぼしているかを
まとめた。展示会は4月、準備は真冬なので、ロケはなるべ
く暖かく、多少でも緑が残る場所でと検討した結果、九州の
宮崎になった。昼間、海水が引いた時に本を建て、ジッと夕
方の満潮を待って撮影、翌朝の干潮までセットはそのままな
ので、夜の海に本の塔が白く浮かんでいた。

Fujii Tamotsu, photographer, took photos for the posters and booklets to be distributed at the exhibition. We created two posters with the sea and a forest symbolizing water and wood, both indispensable elements to make paper, and the tower of white books as a symbol of paper.(P150,151) For the booklet with the theme of paper and the environment, the photos of the fiber of paper from the ancient times and that of vegetables were enlarged to show how paper is made, and incineration and bleaching were visually presented to show how paper is affecting the environment. The exhibition was held in April, and the photographing took place in the middle of winter. We chose Miyazaki in southern Kyushu as the shooting location, which is warmer and has more greenery than any other places. We piled books when the tide was on the ebb in the daytime, and waited until the tide was on the flow in the evening to shoot. We kept the set as it was until the next day, so the white book tower appeared to be floating on the sea in the dark.

1999 TAKEO PAPER SHOW

紙の十字架

4月22日[木]─24日[土] 11:00-20:00 初日は18:30まで 青山スパイラルガーデン&ホール 入場無料 株式会社 竹尾 tel.03-3292-3611

1999 TAKEO PAPER SHOW
紙の十字架

4月22日[木]－24日[土] 11:00－20:00 初日は18:30まで 青山スパイラルガーデン＆ホール 入場無料 株式会社竹尾 tel.03-3292-3611

153

見本帖本店は、紙のショップ兼ショウルーム。西沢立衛さんに設計をお願いし、竹尾のデザインコミッティのメンバーと一緒にコラボレートしてもらった。全体が真っ白な空間に、紙をカラーグラデーションで分類して並べた細いテーブルが11台というシンプルな構成。壁面は天井から床まで全てストック用の引き出しになっており、小さな記号でサインが付いている。東京神田に出現した白い箱に、道行く人も立ち止まり、何だろう?と覗き込む。きっとコンビニより明るいかもしれない。

Mihoncho Honten is a paper shop and showroom of Takeo. Architect Nishizawa Ryue and Takeo's Design Committee members collaborated in designing the interior architecture. In the white interior, 11 narrow tables were placed showing paper grouped by color gradation. The drawers containing paper occupied the wall surfaces from the ceiling to the floor, and a small sign was attached to each drawer.
Passers-by stop in their tracks to look into this white box that has emerged in downtown Kanda. This shop might be brighter than convenience shops.

| | | | | | | | | | | | |
|---|---|---|---|---|---|---|---|---|---|---|---|
| 1 | 1 | | | 1 | O | 1 | 1 | | 1 | P | 1 | 1 |
| 1 | 2 | | | 1 | O | 1 | 2 | | 1 | P | 1 | 2 |
| 1 | 3 | | | 1 | O | 1 | 3 | | 1 | P | 1 | 3 |
| 1 | 4 | | | 1 | O | 1 | 4 | | 1 | P | 1 | 4 |
| 1 | 5 | | | 1 | O | | 5 | | 1 | P | 1 | 5 |
| 1 | 6 | | | | O | 1 | 6 | | 1 | P | 1 | 6 |
| 1 | 7 | | | 1 | O | 1 | 7 | | 1 | P | 1 | 7 |
| 1 | 8 | | | 1 | O | 1 | 8 | | | P | 1 | 8 |
| 1 | 9 | | | 1 | O | 1 | 9 | | 1 | P | 1 | 9 |
| 2 | 0 | | | 1 | O | 2 | 0 | | 1 | P | 2 | 0 |
| 2 | 1 | | | 1 | O | 2 | 1 | | 1 | P | 2 | 1 |
| 2 | 2 | | | 1 | O | 2 | 2 | | 1 | P | 2 | 2 |
| 2 | 3 | | | 1 | O | 2 | 3 | | 1 | P | 2 | 3 |
| 2 | 4 | | | 1 | O | 2 | 4 | | 1 | P | 2 | 4 |
| 2 | 5 | | | 1 | O | 2 | 5 | | 1 | P | 2 | 5 |
| 2 | 6 | | | 1 | O | 2 | 6 | | 1 | P | 2 | 6 |
| 2 | 7 | | | 1 | O | 2 | 7 | | 1 | P | 2 | 7 |
| 2 | 8 | | | 1 | O | 2 | 8 | | 1 | P | 2 | 8 |
| 2 | 9 | | | 1 | O | 2 | 9 | | 1 | P | 2 | 9 |
| 3 | 0 | | | 1 | O | 3 | 0 | | 1 | P | 3 | 0 |
| 3 | 1 | | | 1 | O | 3 | 1 | | 1 | P | 3 | 1 |
| 3 | 2 | | | 1 | O | 3 | 2 | | 1 | P | 3 | 2 |
| 3 | 3 | | | 1 | O | 3 | 3 | | 1 | P | 3 | 3 |
| 3 | 4 | | | 1 | O | 3 | 4 | | 1 | P | 3 | 4 |
| 3 | 5 | | | 1 | O | 3 | 5 | | 1 | P | 3 | 5 |

155

このショップで扱う紙は、ファインペーパーといってポスターやパッケージなどに使用する高級紙。全体で3000種類ある紙を、カラフル、白、マテリアルと大きく三つに分けて選択できる。選んだ紙をカウンターに持って行くと、店員が引き出しから必要な枚数を出してくれる。またそれ以上の大きな紙は店の奥にストックしてあり、頼めば自由な大きさにカットしてくれる。

The paper products here are all high-class paper used for posters and packages. Customers can select from among 3000 kinds of paper classified largely into three groups of Colorful Paper, White Paper and Materials. Upon selection, a customer brings the sample to the counter, and a clerk takes out the required number of sheets from the drawers. Larger sized sheets are stocked in the storage behind the counter. They can cut paper to size, as a customer desires.

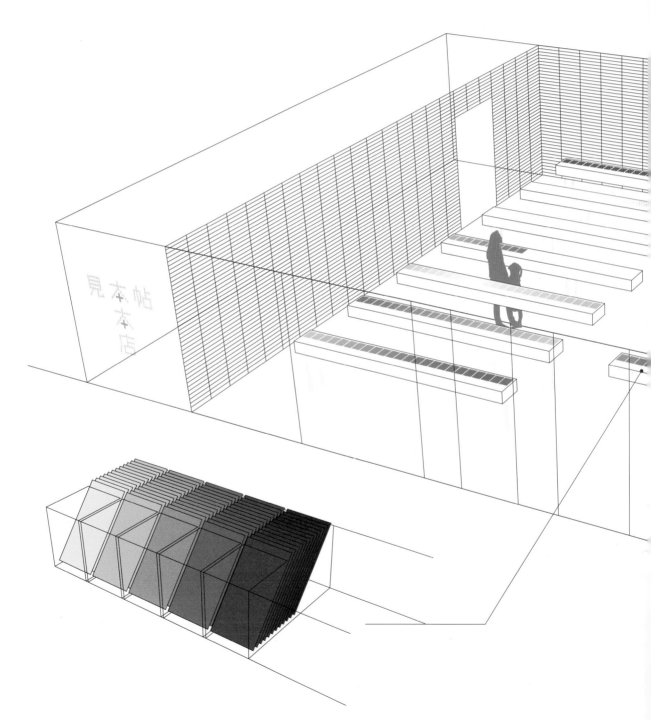

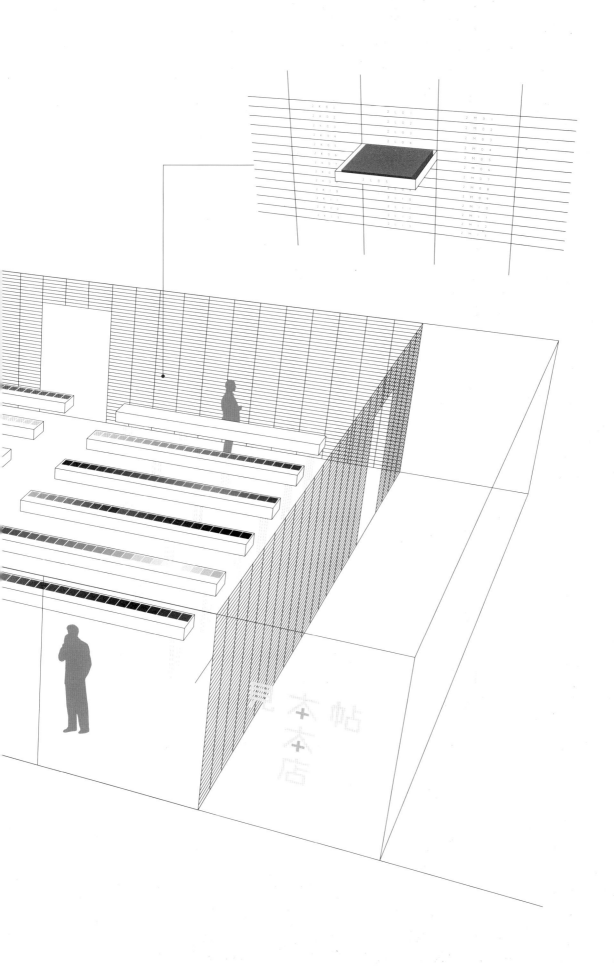

# VISUAL I

空間におけるグラフィックデザインでは、VI（ヴィジュアル アイデンティティー）という、空間の意味を視覚化するプログラムが重要な要素になります。

VIは、空間の名称や目的を人々に明解に伝えるために、空間だけでなく、多様なメディアを使い、独自のアイデンティティーを効果的に表現します。

また、VIはサインシステムと深くリンクして計画することで、体験する人に強い印象を与えます。建物や環境自体が与える包括的な印象より、具体性が高く視覚的なVIが、空間の意志を直接的に伝える効果的なツールとなり得るのです。

VIの構成要素は、目的によって異なります。基本的には、シンボルマーク、ロゴタイプ、カラー、タイプフェイス、場合によってキャラクターやコピーなどから成り立ちます。それらは互いに組み合わせて展開され、平面的にはステーショナリー（封筒、便箋、名刺）、立体的には様々なグッズやノベルティ、そして空間的にはサインシステムなどに応用して展開していきます。

空間は、それ自身のアイデンティティーに、グラフィカルな要素を加えることで、より明解なコンセプションを表現することができるのです。だから美術館と学校では、それぞれの目的や使われ方が違うように、VI開発の方程式も違います。余談ですが、VIに対するユーザーの評価は時として気まぐれです。「カワイイ」が「カッコイイ」より優先する場合や、「メルヘン」が「モダン」より多くの人に共感を得る場合があり得るのです。

望まれることは必要なことであり、デザイナーは多様なニーズに対し、常に答えを出さなくてはなりません。ただユーザーの既成概念をうち破る新たなありかたを提示するエネルギーが、よりよいVI計画に必要であることは言うまでもありません。

For a visual identity (VI) for a space, a program to visualize the meaning of the space is an important element.

A VI uses the space itself and various other media to convey the name and the purpose of the space clearly to the public.

Linking the VI with the sign system will impress the people more strongly. Rather than the impression that a space or a building gives, a concrete and graphic VI may serve as an effective tool to express what the space is.

Elements used for a VI may vary according to the purpose. Basic components include symbol mark, logotype, colors, typeface, and additionally mascot characters and message copy. They are used in combination, and applied to stationery (envelopes, writing pads, visiting cards), various goods and novelties, and sign systems.

With graphical elements, a clearer concept of a space can be presented. As a museum and a school have different purposes, VI development methods for them are different. People's criteria for evaluation are often capricious.

Sometimes, they prefer "cute" to "cool" and "fanciful" to "modern."

Designers must respond to such customers' desires, but at the same time, we should have strong energy to present something novel to break their established ideas in creating a VI.

# DENTITY

日本科学未来館

アートディレクション：廣村正彰
デザイン：廣村正彰、前田豊
建築設計：日建設計・久米設計設計共同企業体
施工：びこう社
クライアント：科学技術振興事業団

National Museum of Emerging
Science and Innovation

art direction : Hiromura Masaaki
design : Hiromura Masaaki, Maeda Yutaka
architect : Nikken Kume Joint Trust
construction : Bikohsha
client : Japan Science and Technology

札幌メディアパーク・スピカ

アートディレクション：廣村正彰
デザイン：廣村正彰、木住野英彰
建築設計：伊坂重春
施工：アドバンス井畑
クライアント：札幌テレビ放送

Sapporo Media Park Spica

art direction : Hiromura Masaaki
design : Hiromura Masaaki,
Kishino Hideaki
architect : Isaka Shigeharu
construction : Advance Ihata
client : The Sapporo Television
Broadcasting

横須賀市立美術館（仮称）

デザイン：廣村正彰、前田豊
建築設計：山本理顕
クライアント：横須賀市

Yokosuka Museum of Art
(provisional name)

design : Hiromura Masaaki,
Maeda Yutaka
architect : Yamamoto Riken
client : Yokosuka City

北野共生システム プロジェクト

アートディレクション：廣村正彰
デザイン：廣村正彰、水野佳史
内装設計：山本理顕
アドバイザー：北野宏明
コーディネーション：山崎あかね
施工管理：美留土
クライアント：科学技術振興事業団

Kitano Symbiotic Systems Project

art direction : Hiromura Masaaki
design : Hiromura Masaaki,
Mizuno Yoshifumi
interior architect : Yamamoto Riken
adviser : Kitano Hiroaki
coordination : Yamazaki Akane
construction management : Build
client : Japan Science and Technology

NATIONAL MUSEUM OF EMERGING SCIENCE AND INNOVATION

日本科学未来館は、VIを決定すると同時に館を象徴する シンボル展示が制作された。直径6.5mのLEDで被われた 球体は、宇宙からの地球の姿を写し出し、館長で宇宙飛行士の 毛利衛さんのイメージと重なって、館の重要なキャラクター になった。グラフィックのシンボルマークは抽象的な表現だが、 このシンボル展示との連動で、認知がスムーズに行われ、グッ ズなどにも展開された。

Upon the determination of the visual identity for the National Museum of Emerging Science and Innovation, the symbolic exhibit was created. The globe with an 6.5-meter diameter covered with LEDs reflected as the earth seen from space. Together with the image of Mohri Mamoru, astronaut and the director of the museum, this symbol became the important character of the museum. Combined with this symbol, the abstract graphic symbol mark was smoothly recognized. Both symbol and mark are now used for souvenirs of the museum.

 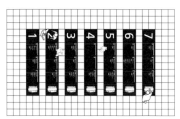 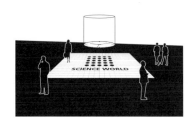

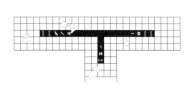 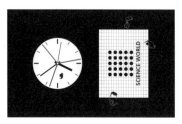 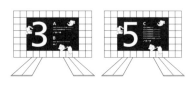

162

サインシステムは事前に2案出した。一つは決定した案で、全体を通し、床面を利用したプラン。建築の持つ透明感や展示が主体の施設の内容を考慮に入れ、なるべく視線を遮らないサインシステムです。必要な情報は床から得られ、それに誘導されて目的に着く。定点のサインは床から壁面に立ち上がり視認性が高い。もう一方のプランは矢印がいっぱいの案で、外装のガラスにも矢印がたくさん表示されている。先方はこれを見て「ムムー、スゴイ」と驚いたが、ボツになった。

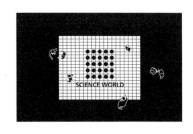 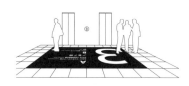 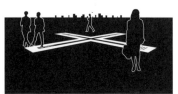

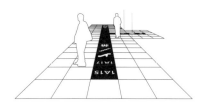 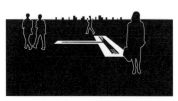 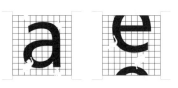

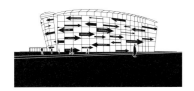 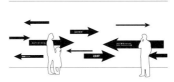 

 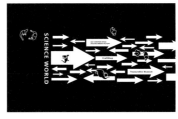 

Two sign system designs were proposed. First proposal was a system using the floors as signboards. This was aimed not to spoil the sense of transparency of the building and not to obstruct the view of the exhibit-centered interior. Signs on the floor would guide the visitors to go to their destinations. On the wall at a turning point, signs would be shown vertically. The other one used arrows as a motif. The exterior glass walls would be covered with graphically presented arrows. The museum staff members were surprised with this idea, but did not take up this design.

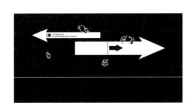 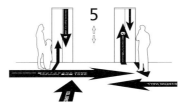 

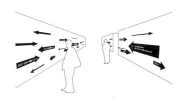  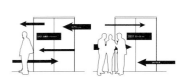

館全体のサインシステムは、床面に表示された情報に基づき誘導される。それは外構から始まっており、エントランス、駐車場、バスの停留所、ゆりかもめの駅、カフェテラス等を誘導する。夜の効果も考慮し、内照式になっており、サインが認知できるように表面は、透明ガラスで仕上げているが水分が付着すると滑りやすく、危険なのでガラスの粉末をドットのパターンで蒸着させている。何回か摩擦係数のテストを行い、ドットの大きさやピッチを決めたが、その数値を計出するのに、どこの誰に依頼したら良いか、さっぱり見当も付かず、施工を担当した大兼さんが、専門に研究されている大学教授を探し出してくれた。

Signs installed on the floor guide the visitors from the exterior of the museum, to the entrance, parking area, bus stops, station, cafe terrace, etc. They are lit from inside to have an effect for illumination. Glass is used for the surface to express a transparent feeling. It is easy to change information. To prevent the visitors to slip when water attaches to the surface, dotted glass grains are printed with vacuum evaporation to enhance friction. We did not know anyone who can calculate the value of friction, and Ohkane in charge of construction looked for a professor specializing in this field.

床面のサインシステムでは通常のものに比べ、多量の文字情報は認知しにくい為、ピクトグラムや記号化したアルファベットを使い、瞬間的に識別できるように考えた。文字もなるべく大きく扱うことで見やすくしたが、なかなか書体がしっくりこないので、途中でアルファベットをオリジナルで創ることにした。フルティガーを骨格に角を少し落としたタイプフェイスは、未来館にピッタリだった。

Signs on the floor can hold fewer letters. Pictograms and symbolized letters are used. We tried to use large size letters, but as I was not satisfied with the existing alphabet typefaces, I decided to create a new style. The typeface created based on an existing style was just fit to this museum.

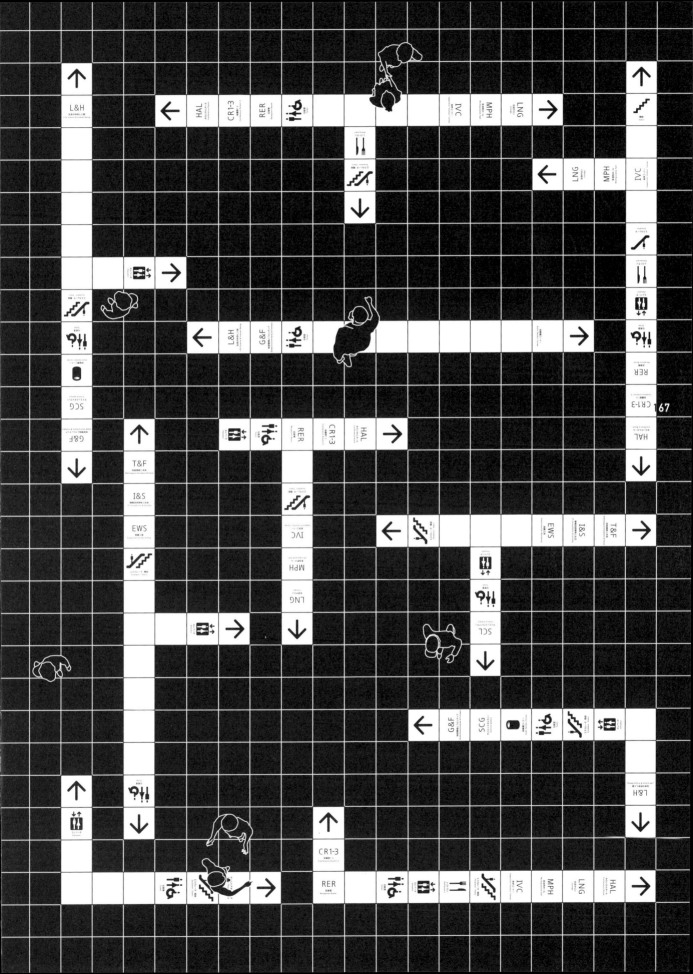

168

巷でも、地面や床面の情報表示を目にすることが結構ある。一般的には道路上に描かれた注意書きや方向指示などであるが、漫画や劇画などの仮想現実の世界では床面は表現の対象として頻繁に利用されている。それは地面や床が感覚的にいつの時代でも、人間と大地という地球的信頼感で結ばれているからで、その安心できる大地を加工することで、意識的に未来感を演出しているのである。現実には未来館のようにメインの案内情報が床面に表示されている施設はなかなか他にない。一般的な概念や常識から考えるとサインとしては効率的ではないからだが、新たな可能性を模索、挑戦することが、日本科学未来館の基本理念でもあり、ここの館長である毛利さんの理解もあってなんとか実現化した。しかし見慣れない方式のため苦情は多い。結果的に後付けで壁面にベタベタ紙のサインを追加するのではなく、来訪者にちゃんとシステムを理解してもらうことが、未来館としての正しい姿勢だと説明している。

There are signs given on the ground or floor. The most common are signs drawn on the roads such as warning words, destinations and arrows. People are accustomed to these signs. There are few, yet, that public facilities utilize the floors to give important information. From a general concept, using the floor as a signboard is not realistic and effective. However, exploring a frontier and challenging the fixed ideas are the basic concept this museum, and Director Mohri also agreed with the use of this system. In cartoons and comics with narratives, the ground or the floor is often used as the object for expression. It is because the ground and the floor are associated with the earth and give a feeling of security to people at all times. By drawing on the ground, cartoonists consciously create a futuristic atmosphere in their works. As this is new to a museum, there have been many complaints. Instead of adding paper signs, I tell the museum staff that the right thing to do for this futuristic museum is to encourage the visitors to get accustomed to the system.

日本科学未来館
NATIONAL MUSEUM OF EMERGING SCIENCE AND INNOVATION

VIは、日本科学未来館の存在、意味、役割を世に広く知らしめる為のツールであり、幅広い年齢や職業、多様な国々、言語を超えて共通のイメージが伝えられるようにシステムを組まなくてはならない。シンボルマークは「ブルーオーブ」と呼ばれ、VIシステムの中核の役割を担っている。マークは青い円とラインでできており、地球とネットワークをイメージしている。広がりを持たせるため、下部をカットした展開もあり、可変的で能動的なVIを目指した。

A visual identity (VI) is a tool to make a project and its significance and functions known to the public. It must be designed so that a wide range of people can share a common image regardless of their ages, occupations, nationalities and languages. The symbol mark named "Blue Orb" plays the central VI role for the Museum of Emerging Science and Innovation. This mark is composed of a blue circle and lines in the image of the earth and networks. In another application, the lower portion of the mark is cut. I intended to create a changeable and active VI.

毛利　衛

館　　長
宇宙飛行士

日本科学未来館

〒135-0064 東京都江東区青海2丁目41番地3
Tel 03-0000-0000　Fax 03-0000-0000
http://www.miraican.jst.go.jp
mohri@miraican.jst.go.jp

VIの制作では、マークの存在が重要だと考え、多めのプランを試作して、早い時期に関係者に公開した。通常事前に2～3案に絞り込んで、ある程度の展開も進めた上でプレゼンテーションするのだが、初期の頃は決済者や決済の機構が見えにくかったので、担当現場レベルの方々に見てもらい、多くの人の協力を取り付けたかった。特にお役所の場合、女性の意見はとても重要で強力な味方になるので、アンケートを取ってもらい、段階を踏んだ。結果的に、館長に直接説明することができて、皆と同じ方向に決まった。

In designing the visual identity, the mark is an important element. So I prepared many ideas at an early time, and showed them to interested people who were involved in the starting up of this museum, because the decision makers or decision-making mechanism were not clear at the beginning. In the case of government facilities, women's voices are important. Therefore, a survey was conducted asking which mark designs would be favored among women. Finally, Director Mohri agreed to the result of the survey.

MeSci ミーサイ

NATIONAL MUSEUM OF EMERGING SCIENCE AND INNOVATION

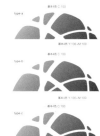

無事オープンして、少しホッとしてると毛利館長から日本科学未来館を、MeSci(ミーサイ)というネーミングで呼べるようにしたいとの意向があった。MeSciとは英語館名のNATIONAL MUSEUM OF EMERGING SCIENCE AND INNOVATION の略称とミー アンド サイエンスという二つの意味がある。たしかに和文の館名で呼ぶのは形式的で固いのでこのプランは賛成だが、問題があった。商標が取れない、アルファベットでは類似に抵触するので、苦肉の策でカタカナ併記で出発することになった。

When the museum was officially opened, and all the people involved were sharing a feeling of relief, Director Mohri wanted to give a nickname of "MeSci" to this museum. It stands for the Museum of Emerging Science, and "Me and Science." I agreed to his idea because its title in Japanese is very formal. A problem was found that in Japan we cannot register trademarks in alphabet, as the last resort, MeSci (mi-sai) in alphabet and the Japanese phonetic sign was registered.

MeSciは、国内は元より海外の研究機関、科学館などと常に連携をしている。活動内容を広く知ってもらい、世界中にネットワークを広げるために、印刷物やウェブサイトはとても重要なツールになる。グラフィックデザインもなるべくシンプルに制作して、世界基準にした方が良い。

MeSci is linked with research institutes and science museums both in Japan and other countries. Printed materials and website contents are playing an important role to publicize the activities of the museum and to expand its network worldwide. Simple graphics are favorable to publicize it on the international level.

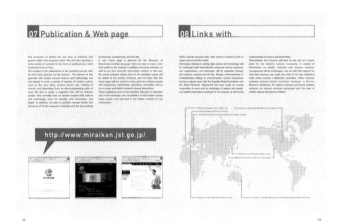

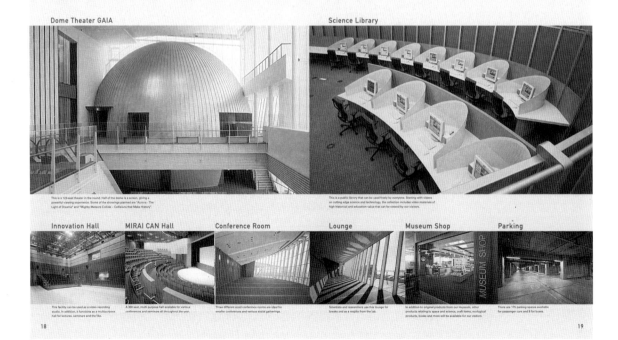

The distinctive landscaping, illumination for the exterior and interior of the museum,
art and signs planning also are based on a total design concept

## Landscaping

The theme is coexistence and fusion of science, nature and people. At the entrance of the museum, the rolling configuration of the land is used like sculpture to suggest the appearance of molecules colliding, bouncing and fusing. The outdoor exhibit area is structured like waves, showing the waves of light, sound and electrons created from technological and scientific research.

## Illumination

Light generated by the wind, the sun and the moon is represented. This exterior is lit by wind power, and the look of the "Wind Light" can be changed subtly by changing the force of the wind. The open side of the exhibit zone is lit by "Moonlight", a bluish-white light coming from the "moon", which is the gently rounded surface of the ceiling. Finally, the Exhibit Spaces and Through Halls are filled with "Sunlight" even after the sun has gone down.

## Art

From the entrance along the staircase is found a quiet work of art consisting of about 150 tree leaves made from brass frames and acrylic boards that looks like washi, floating in space and rising up lightly. The motif is of tree leaves as the key to nature's energy, and the work creates a sense of continuity in the large open space.

## Signs

The main feature of the signs (showing the locations of various places in the museum) is the fact that we have, as much as possible, done away with conventional signposts and the like, and placed the signs in the floor. By displaying information in the floor, we ensure that visits to the museum will have the experience of receiving information from a completely new angle as they walk on the signs to their destinations.

## **11** Design

The concept for the design of MeSci was to create a space for interaction between science and technology, and people, and among people. Many inventive measures have been taken in the design and technological areas to make the museum an appropriate space to experience cutting edge science and technology.

### Exterior

### Entrance

### Exhibit Space

### Exhibit Space

Environmentally Symbiotic Housing

Shinkai 6500

# THE EARTH ENVIRONMENT & FRONTIERS

Over a long period of time, we have used the resources of this enormous system called earth to build a material civilization. Our activities have spread as far as space in the 20th century. Upon our arrival in space we saw how far-reaching the human influence has become and realized there are limits to the resources upon which we depend.

Humans are now challenged to build new technological systems that will exist in harmony with the earth's environment. We are working to convert to systems that not only consumes resources but also recycles them.

Space exploration, too, has expanded from the solar system to the galaxy and the galactic cosmos, and with this, our awareness and sense of values in relation to the earth have changed, as well. In this area, we present the theme of how to coexist with the earth, our oasis in space, and how to incorporate that for our future society.

We also encourage innovative approaches to the many challenges facing all forms of life and to our planet generally.

### 1. Towards Synergy with the Environment
Here we discover effective methods of using energy and new technological systems,to inspire us to consider new ways for humans to interact with our environment.

### 2. Space and Time
We introduce new challenges posed by the frontier of outer space and the "inner space" frontier of the oceans.

### 3. Exploration
We present plans for exploration of our solar system as well as leading edge research into solar measurement. We also present subterranean research which reveals the secrets of history of the earth and our moon.

### 4. Extreme Environments
Here, we aim for a deeper understanding of the world of the ocean depths, which are inextricably linked to the global environment and the birth of life, and the new human sphere of activity, space.

## Some of the Items on Exhibit

**Environmentally Symbiotic Housing**
The component elements of cutting-edge symbiosis housing and traditional Japanese housing are combined and contrasted in a full-sized housing model. We discover how to live in harmony with nature, taking from the wisdom and technology of both old and new.

**Shinkai 6500**
A life-size reproduction of Shinkai 6500, the manned submersible research vehicle that has gone deeper than any other. You can enter the cockpit and experience the feeling of exploration, and the advanced technology that makes exploration under extreme conditions possible.

**Frontier Lab**
This offers a virtual experience of interpreting materials and observation data from the front line of research on space, the oceans and the earth.

Environmental Technologies, Exploring the Solar System, Ocean-Controlled Environments, Motion Ride : The Dreamer, etc.

## Advisors

Dr. Yoichi Kaya [Chair]
Director-General, Research Institute of Innovative Technology for the Earth

Dr. Hajime Akimoto
Program Director, Frontier Research System for Global Change

Mr. Toshihiko Kikuyama
Invited Scientist, National Space Development Agency of Japan

Dr. Yoshiharu Doi
Prof., Department of Innovative and Engineered Materials, Tokyo Institute of Technology

Dr. Takafumi Matsui
Prof.,Graduate School of Frontier Sciences, The University of Tokyo

Mr. Yasunori Matogawa
Prof., Office of External Relations/Director, kagoshima Space Center, The Institute of Space and Astronautical Science

Mr. Hiroshi Hotta
Scientific Advisor to the President, Japan Marine Science & Technology Center

Dr. Koichi Yamada
Prof., Department of Fine Materials Engineering, Shinshu University

10

11

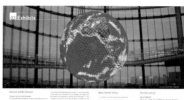

# LIFE SCIENCES

Sequencing Puzzle

Exhibits

### 1. Genome

### 2. Brain

### 3. Medicine

## Some of the Items on Exhibit

**Close Up of Body Mechanisms**

**The Development of the Brain**

**Using Cutting-Edge Technology to Replicate the Human Body**

## Advisors

Dr. Ichiro Kanazawa (Chair)
Prof. and Chairman, Department of Neurology, The University of Tokyo Hospital

Dr. Motoya Katsuki
Director-General, National Institute for Basic Biology, Okazaki National Research Institute

Dr. Yoji Ikehara
Prof. and Head, National Institute of Genetics

Dr. Yasufumi Ogihara
Emeritus Prof., Tokyo Women's Medical University

Mr. Hiromasa Hirai
Associate Prof., The University of Tokyo Hospital

---

PINO The Humanoid Robot

MIRAICAN MAGLEV

# INNOVATION & THE FUTURE

The human being has discovered one new world after another, from milli to micron, and further to the nano-level of technology, called nanotechnology. During the process of reaching the nano level, a new technology of building extremely small machines, called micromachines, was born. At the same time, the development of robots has been actively pursued, giving us machines that move like living things and are versatile, flexible, and autonomous, while employing the characteristics of computerization. LSI, lasers and optical electronics have emerged from the theoretical world of quantum physics into the new world of quantum technology of the future. In addition, the development of superconductive and other technologies which place a smaller burden on the environment is a major trend of the 21st century. We present the latest developments based on the remarkable advances in these technologies, and focusing on nanotechnology, micromachines, robotics, superconductive technology, and the new relationships between humans and technologies.

### 1. Nanotechnology

We explore today's nanotechnology in LSI and lasers, optical electronics and the like, with a dynamic introduction to the magnificent nanotech story, leading from the quantum world to the quantum technology of the future.

### 2. Micromachine

Here you can make micromachines move with your own hands, and actually experience the micro world. We also investigate what kinds of things will be made possible by micromachines from now on, with a look at the many future possibilities in a variety of fields.

### 3. Robot

We present the cutting-edge robot technology of Japan, the world's leader in this field, and display working models. We also look into the fundamental question of what robots are, and the relationship between robots and humans.

### 4. Superconductor

Superconductivity is called the base technology for the future - what exactly is this phenomenon? You can enjoy experiencing the magic of how magnetic levitation works as we consider its new possibilities and its future.

## Some of the Items on Exhibit

**LSI-A City Built with Nanotechnology**
A combined presentation of models and images helps you to discover the cutting edge of LSI, through which you can experience the world of nanoelectronics.

**Operate a Micromachine**
As you move the machines yourself, you can enjoy modeling work on a micro scale. This experience brings an understanding of the micromachine mechanism.

**Robot World**
We present a world - Robot World - where several types of robots perform. Seeing robots actually moving makes us think about the relationship between humans and their new creation, the robot.

Quantum Effects and Nanotechnology, Micromachine Lab, Magnetism and Levitation, Robot Functions, MIRAI CAN MAGLEV, etc.

## Advisors

Dr. Koichi Kitazawa (Chair)
Prof., Graduate School of Frontier Sciences, The University of Tokyo Earth

Dr. Hiroaki Kitano
Senior Researcher, Sony Computer Science Laboratories Inc.

Dr. Hiroyuki Sakaki
Prof., Institute of Industrial Science, The University of Tokyo

Mr. Hiroshi Nakashima
Deputy Director General, Technical Research and Development Division, Central Japan Railway Co.

Dr. Hiroyuki Fujita
Prof., Institute of Industrial Science, The University of Tokyo

SAPPORO MEDIA PARK SPICA

Sapporo Media Park
spica

184

電話コーナー Telephone

→

EV
エレベーター
Elevator

階段
Stairs

化粧室 Restroom

B1
O
B2

スピカは、札幌に新しい表現の場としてできた全天候型の
ホールである。設計は伊坂重春さん。天井が開閉する特殊
な設計は、夏期の重要な自然光を最大限活用するための
アイデアである。多目的なホールは可変的に利用されるので、
サインシステムもフレキシブルに考えた。

Sapporo Media Park Spica is an all-weather hall built
in Sapporo, Hokkaido.　Architect Isaka Shigeharu
designed it to have a movable roof that can open to
allow natural light to enter in the summer.　As the
hall is multi-purpose and is used for many
performances using different stage settings, I
designed the sign system flexibly.

186

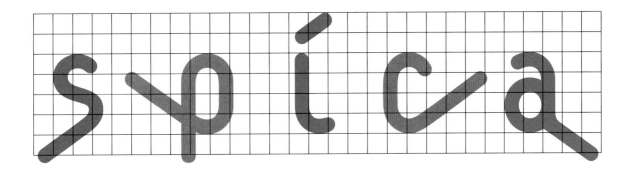

サインシステムの開発で始まったプロジェクトだったが、愛称募集の審査がキッカケとなり、VIとキャラクターの開発にも関わることになった。母体でもあるデベロッパーの、札幌テレビが使っている「さっちゃん」というキャラクターを「スピカ」に変更し、このホール共々メディアの顔にする作戦である。

The project began with the development of the sign system. Later, I worked as a judge to select a nickname for the facility, and the development of the VI and the character was also assigned to me. It was agreed that the existing character "Sacchan" of the developer of Spica, the Sapporo TV, would be used for Spica by only renaming it "Spica." This character is now used for both TV and the hall.

メディアにおけるキャラクターの役割とは、メディアのメディア化である。シンボルに記号化されたキャラクターは、世代や地域の格差をまざまざと露呈するメディアにおけるブラックボックスであり、コミュニケーションレスな部分を吸収するショックアブソーバーなのである。それには絶対的な「カワイイ」と「カンタン」が必要になる。キティ、ドラエモン、ミッキー、ミフィーどれもその条件を備えている。だからスピカもシンプルな造形、世代を超えて愛されるかわいさ、メリハリのあるカラーリングなどを考えながら進めることにした。

190

A symbol character for the media is a medium to connect different generations and different classes of people who otherwise will not communicate with each other. The absolute preconditions for successful characters are "cute" and "simple." Kitty, Doraemon, Mickey and Miffy are all meeting these requirements. We developed simple and lovable forms for the Spica character, and gave it clear and bright colors.

YOKOSUKA MUSEUM OF ART

突然、建築家の山本理顕さんから電話があり、2007年に
オープンする横須賀美術館のロゴを作って欲しいとのこと。
建築は?と聞くと、これからとか。そしてオープンするまで使
いたい、という条件でした。まだ先が長く、実体が見えにくい
プロジェクトなので、市民と共有できるヴィジュアル アイデ
ンティティが必要だという。山本さんが考えたアイデアでと
ても共感し、ロゴTシャツやシールに展開した。

One day, architect Yamamoto Riken called asking me
to develop the logo for the Yokosuka Museum of Art
to be open in 2007.   I asked him about its construction,
and he replied, "Not yet."  He wanted to use the logo
until the museum is opened.  As this project was still
in the planning process, no concrete image had been
formed, and he needed a visual identity that can be
shared with Yokosuka city people.  As his ideas were
agreeable, I prepared a few designs which are
currently used for T-shirts and seals.

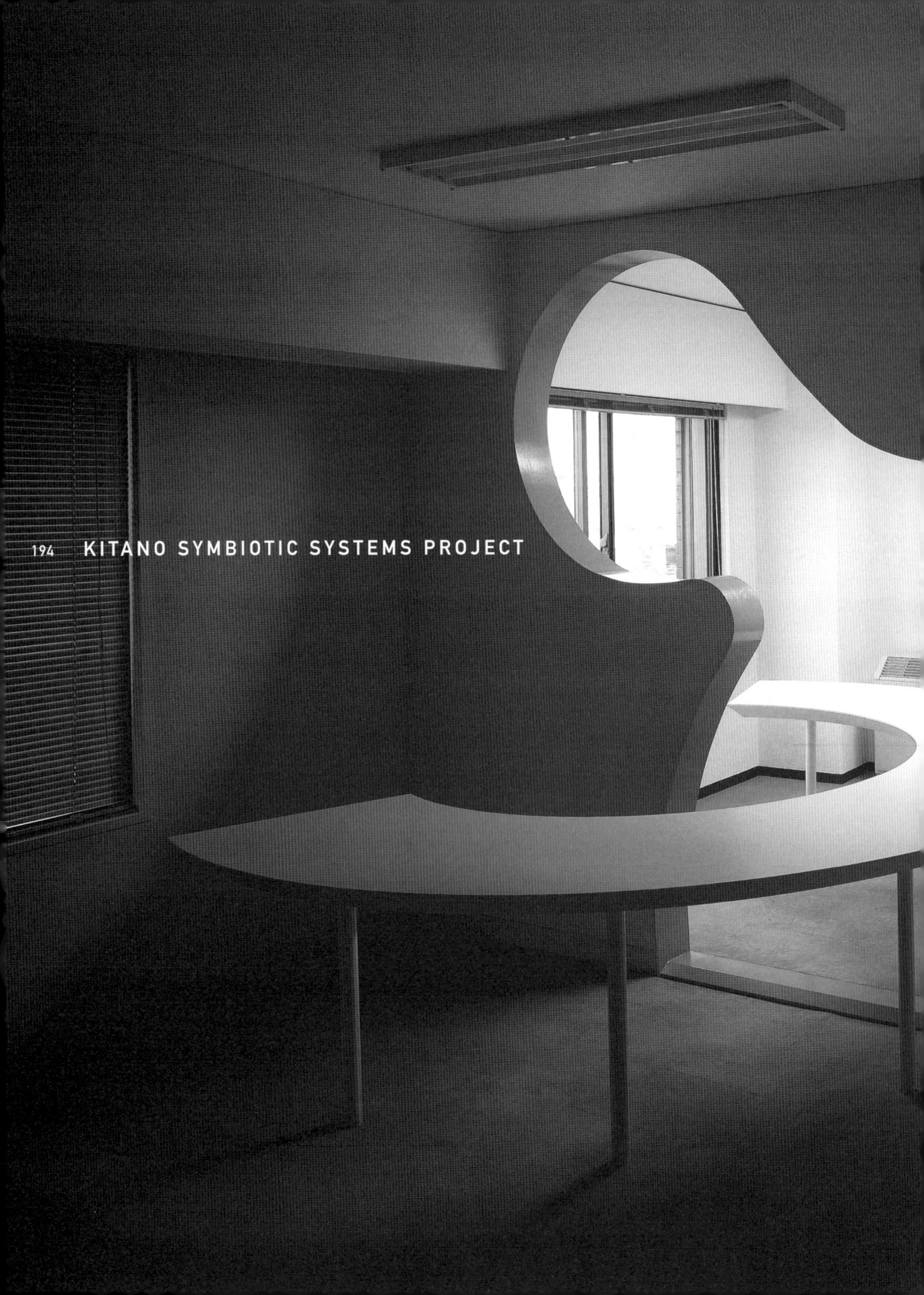

# 194 KITANO SYMBIOTIC SYSTEMS PROJECT

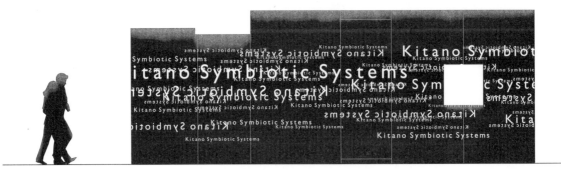

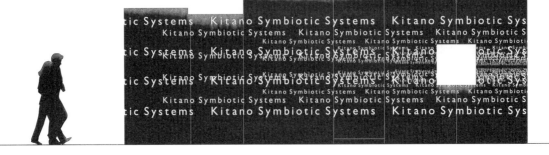

北野宏明さんは、システムバイオロジーと人工知能の科学者である。科学技術振興事業団より5年の期限付きで、東京原宿に研究所を開設することになり、VIを制作することになった。科学者だがクリエイティブなことが大好きな方なので、プレゼンも議論が尽きず難航した。しかしそれは常に楽しいディスカッションであった。決まったマークは有機的で増殖をイメージする形で、キャラクターのようでもあった。設計の山本さんと北野さんが、壁面をマークの形で抜いたり、ロゴタイプを使い、廊下をグラフィカルに演出した。

Kitano Hiroaki is a scientist specializing in system biology and artificial intelligence. His office, Kitano Symbiotic Institute, was opened in a fashionable district in Tokyo for a 5-year term commissioned by the Japan Science and Technology Corp. My presentations for its VI were tough, but there were exciting moments of discussion at the same time. Scientist as he may be, he likes creative things. The mark finally determined had an organic form with the image of biological propagation, and it could serve as the character for the institute. Architect Yamamoto and Dr. Kitano made the hole in the wall in the shape of the mark. I decorated the corridor walls graphically by using the logotypes.

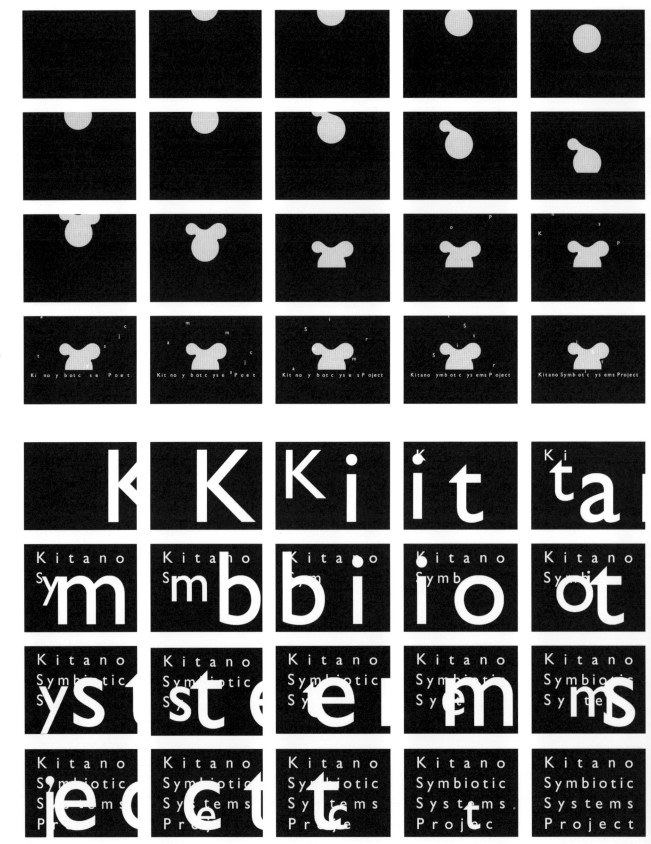

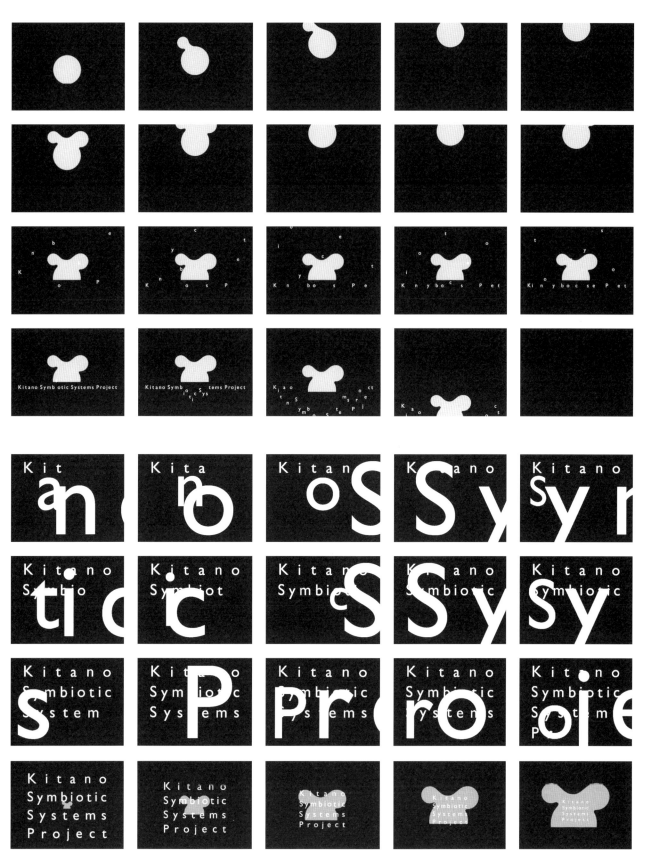

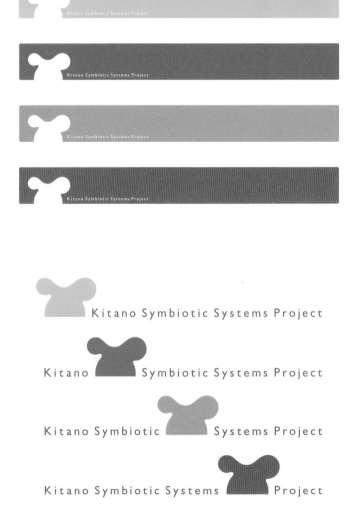

VIの展開も研究施設らしからぬカワイイ感じのものになった。海外の研究機関との連絡や、学会での発表の時、インパクトのあるものにしたかったという北野さんの希望を少しは叶えられたような気がする。玄関にプロジェクターでシンボルをパタパタ漫画のような動きを付け、投影した。

The VI for this institute was also developed with a friendly feeling for a scientific research institute. Dr. Kitano desired to have something that would give impact when he communicated with colleagues in other countries, or when he presented his research findings at academic meetings. I feel I could have met his desire to some extent. At the entrance hall, we installed a projector to project the symbol like a motion picture.

## 工学とデザインの関係は

### 北野宏明 × 廣村正彰

デザインで伝える共通認識

廣村：「ERATO 北野共生システムプロジェクト」ではVIとサインの仕事をさせていただきました。北野さんが策定委員を務めていた「公立はこだて未来大学」でサイン計画を担当しましたから、これが北野さんとは二つ目の仕事になりますね。

北野：「ERATO」は5年間の限定プロジェクトであるため、早く立ち上げて、しかも研究員が必死になって研究に突っ走れるような環境を設定する必要があったんです。そのためには立地も含め、環境は非常に重要でした。内装は山本理顕さんにお願いして、ガチガチの研究所ではない、普通じゃないものをということで、かなり実験的な試みをしました。たとえば、全ての壁は蛍光灯が仕込んであるライティングウォールで、プロジェクターで投影したり、自由に書いたり消したりできるよう加工したガラスです。他にもさまざまな工夫をしましたが、内装が見えてきた時、エントランスとマークのデザインをどうするかとなって、それで廣村さんにお願いしますということになったんです。

廣村：ロゴマークや独自のツールをつくってビジュアル化することで、そこにある皆の意志がはっきりと見えてくるんです。北野さんが抱いているイメージを共通認識として捉えやすくすることができる。

北野：エントランスも大きな意味がありました。外部の人向けというよりも、内部の人向けにすごくカッコいいものにしたかったんです。というのは、ここで仕事をする研究者たちは毎日そこを通り抜けて仕事につくわけで、そこがすごいということは、口先で「すごいことをやるんだ」というよりずっと効果があると考えたんですね。

曖昧な形と自由な発想

廣村：マークもずいぶん試行錯誤を繰り返しましたよね。最初はロボットや遺伝子を形にしなければいけないのではないかと、いわば固く考えていたんです。アイキャッチになるようなビジュアルをと試行していたのですが、「そういうものじゃない」という話になっていって、今のようにかなり不定型で自由な可能性を持ったものに変わっていった。

北野：最初はもっとシャープなものがいいかなとも悩んだんですが、なぜか毎回案が出てきて検討していくなかで、必ず最後まで落とされずに生き残ったのがこれだった。ちなみに、この形に何があるのかと訊ねたら、廣村さんは「実は意味はない」と答えていました。

廣村：いろいろな意味のあるマークも提案したけれど、なぜかたまたまないのが残った。

## Common Perception Transmitted by Design

Hiromura: I designed the Visual Identity and signs for the ERATO Kitano Symbiotic Systems Project. I worked on the sign system for the Future University-Hakodate with which you were a member of the Assessment Committee. So, the ERATO was the second occasion that I worked with you.

Kitano: Since the ERATO is a five-year project, we needed to establish our office quickly, and we had to prepare an environment that would encourage researchers to devote themselves deliberately in the research work. The environment of our office was important, including its location. I asked Yamamoto Riken to design the interior and we agreed to make something unusual for a scientific research institute. We attempted some experimental devices. For example, all the walls were made to serve as lights as well as walls. We used processed glass for the surfaces, and installed fluorescent lamps behind the glass surfaces. We can now project images on the wall, or we can write on it with a felt pen freely and erase easily. There are some other new devices. When the interior design was almost finished, we began to think about the design of the entrance and the mark, and asked you to design the mark.

Hiromura: By having a logo mark and other visible tools, the intention of the project organizers can be clearly presented. Your intention of the project can be conveyed and easily shared by others inside the organization.

Kitano: The entrance also had important meaning. I wanted to make it something great not only for visitors but also for our staff researchers who come through it every morning to go to their office rooms. It had to be inspirational so that each time they pass it, they would think "I am doing something great here." It would be more effective than for me to tell them that we are going to do something great.

## Ambiguous Form and Free Conception

Hiromura: We came through a long trial-and-error process until we decided on the mark. I first thought rigidly that I had to design a robot or a gene symbolically into an eye-catching mark. But through our discussions, we came to conclude that it should not be like that, and at the end, the mark became something that does not have any defined shape but that can be defined freely.

Kitano: I also thought that something sharp would be good. But while we were

普通、マークをつくる時には、シンボリックであったり、いろいろ意味があるものなんですが、これにはそういうものがなかった。逆に、だからこそ残ったのかもしれない。

北野：表参道という場所から、まず色が決まっていきましたね。

廣村：一般的には科学というと、色はだいたいブルー系に落ち着くんです。でも、このプロジェクトには大学院生など若い人が多い。若々しい色でいきたいと思いました。

北野：色がこれだから、形も暖かな形がいいと言われて「なるほど」と思った。遺伝子など、中身を表現したマークだとイメージが固定され過ぎるし、いろいろなことをしている場であることを表現したいという部分もありました。ならば、中途半端に説明的であるよりも、わからないけれど面白いほうがいいやと思って腹を括ったんですよ。

廣村：話し合いのなかで、マークがどんどんキャラクター化して、そのまま展開へと発展していきました。一つのことから、北野さんはどんどん自分で自由に発想していった。

北野：話しながら、封筒はこれ、名刺はこれ、組織を表す時にはこう使おう、と使い方のシステムもいっしょに決めていきましたよね。

廣村：僕はバラバラと「こういうのも面白いよ」と出していく。整理するのは北野さん。つまりディレクターですよね。提案すると、必ず何か付加価値を持って返してくれるから、僕らも触発されて作業する。作業と、それに対する返答とがキャッチボールのように繰り返されてできていった。「そうか、そういう風にまとめていったら面白いな」と。

204

ヒューマノイド「ピノ」のデザイン

廣村：ところで、北野さんが携わっている先端技術の分野では日本は先進国ですか。

北野：それなりに競争力のある分野ではありますよね。ただ、どの分野をどの国と比べるかによって状況は多少異なってきます。バイオだったら日本にももちろん優秀な人はいるにせよ、アメリカやヨーロッパに比べればかなり弱いし、ロボットならかなり競争力がある。特に二足歩行へのこだわりは、日本はすごいものがありますし、実際にかなり進んでいると言っていいと思います。

廣村：先日、ロボカップ2002が九州であったと聞きましたが。

北野：福岡ドームで約12万人来場しました。

廣村：僕らが見ていても面白い。あれを見ていて思ったのですが、ロボットにはデザインがとても重要なのだと。もしかしたら科学はデザインで変わっていくこともあるのかもしれないと感じたのですが。

北野：あると思いますよ。一方では純粋自然科学の生物学のように蛋白質の生成だとか、遺伝子の解明などのようにデザインの余地がないものもあります。たとえば製薬会社の研究にはデザイン的なものを導入してもコストが膨れるだけですからね。しかし一方、ロボットのように外見のデザインが非常に重要になってしまうジャンルもあるのです。

making selections from among the proposals you had presented for a number of times, the one that survived selection was this one. I asked you what this form meant, and your answer was "No, there's no meaning."

Hiromura: I proposed many marks with meanings, but it happened that a mark design without any meaning was finally selected. Usually, when I design a mark, it symbolizes something, or it suggests some meaning, but in this case, I had nothing like that. It may have been selected because it had no meaning in it.

Kitano: The color was determined first, reflecting the environment of Omote Sando where it is located which is one of the most fashionable districts in Tokyo.

Hiromura: Blue is usually used for scientific institutes. But the staff members of this project were postgraduate students and other young people, so I chose bright youthful colors.

Kitano: You suggested that the shape should be something soft to go with the colors. If we expressed the contents of our project, like genes, in the mark, the image would be fixed. I wanted to symbolize that we were doing many things. Then, I made up my mind to use something interesting rather than an explanatory one, even though I did not see its meaning.

Hiromura: After we selected the mark, it became like the character of the institute. You developed its use in many ways.

Kitano: Yes, while we were talking, I decided to use this for the envelope, this for our cards, this for representing the organization, and so on. We developed the system for its use.

Hiromura: I showed my designs, and you sorted them out and organized them. You were the director. When I proposed a design, you returned it with added value, and I was inspired with it and went on to the next step of my work. Such interactions were repeated, and I realized that the way we were taking was an interesting process.


Design of Humanoid PINO


Hiromura: By the way, is Japan a leading country in the advanced technology that you are engaged in?

Kitano; It is certainly a field that Japan is quite competitive. But it varies from one specialization to another. In biological technology, there are a few excellent researchers in Japan but we can hardly rival the United States and Europe. But in robotics, we have competitive strength. In particular, Japanese researchers are strongly concerned about developing two-leg walking robots. I can say we are advanced in this field.

Hiromura: I heard RoboCup 2002 was held in Kyushu some days ago.

Kitano: It was held at the Fukuoka Dome and attracted 120,000 visitors.

Hiromura: I enjoyed watching it on TV. It was very interesting. I thought that

廣村：北野さんが開発したロボット「ピノ」もデザインが大きな意味を持っているように思いました。

北野：「ピノ」は技術的にはヒューマノイドの最もローエンドを意識的に狙ったものです。秋葉原で買った部品を東急ハンズに図面とともに持ち込んで加工すれば組めてしまうという、かなりふざけたことを言っているくらいですから。それでもとりあえず動く。デザインには結構力を入れていまして、「宇宙船に乗ったピノキオ」というストーリーまである。ピノキオの物語というのは、人間になれない物語ですよね。ロボットも同じです。SFなどから想像すると人間を凌ぐ怖いものというイメージがつきまといますが、そんなものは存在しないし、非常に不完全なものです。その不完全性というのか、弱さというのを表現して、今までのロボット技術ではあまりスポットが当てられていなかった側面を「ピノ」というローエンドのヒューマノイドを通じて表わしたかったのです。

廣村：たしか生まれた時に足形を取るとか、意識的にストーリーをつくるために、いろいろなことをやっていましたよね。

206　外形デザインはイメージの決め手

北野：ある意味、これは一つのロボット開発の方向性だと思います。ロボットは日常に触れるものですから、見た目がすごく大切です。新しい存在として、人間との距離感がどう設定されるかは、見た目のデザインがすごく重要になってくる。しかし、そうした方向性はこれまであまり研究されて来ていなかったんですね。たとえば車輪で動くようなロボットだと、機能から形が決まってきますからデザインの余地はあまりないし、デザインしても面白くない。しかしヒューマノイドやSONYの「アイボ」のようなものにはデザインの余地がかなり大きくなってきます。そこで「ピノ」ではデザインにかなり力を入れて一生懸命やってみようと考えました。

廣村：イメージを伝達するということが、開発の意図を明解にするという意味で、外装というのは重要な役割を果たしたということでしょうか。

北野：かなりの決定打となりました。フレームとしての外観だけだったら「ああ、そう」というだけで終わってしまう。ところがあの形があるからこそ意味が伝わるんです。コストの問題も含め、狙っている技術レベルも、非常にローエンドのロボットですから、たとえばHONDAの「ASIMO」のようにピシッと歩けるわけではありません。もしも「ピノ」が1m50もあるようなものでフラフラ歩いていたら、怖いですよ。しかし、「ピノ」は70cmしかない、いわば1歳半の子どもくらいの大きさです。1歳半ならフラフラしていても違和感はありませんし、部材的なことからいってもその大きさがちょうどフィットしました。

廣村：「ピノ」を見ていて、何でこんなに愛おしいんだろう、と思ったんです。おそらく、そのサイズと形状から来るイメージが、無意識的にピノキオの物語を想像し、不完全なものに対するある種の共感を呼んだのではないかと思います。

design is essential in making a robot. Science may be changed by design.

Kitano: It is possible. In biology as a purely natural science, there is no room for designers to be a part of the process, be it the generation of protein or the explication of genes. If design is introduced into the research of a pharmaceutical company, it would only inflate the cost. But there is a genre such as robotics where appearance is very important, and where designers can become involved.

Hiromura: For the robot "Pino" that you developed, design played an important role.

Kitano: PINO is a humanoid made intentionally with a low-end technique. We often joke that we buy parts at Akihabara electric shopping center and bring them together with a drawing to the Tokyu Hands do-it-yourself shop, where you can make an assembly kit. It moves any way. But we emphasized design in this product. We also prepared a story "Pinocchio on a spaceship." Pinocchio is a story that this wooden doll cannot become a human. Robots cannot become humans either. If you read science fiction, you may think that robots surpass human power and ability, but there is no such a thing in the real world, because robots are imperfect. I wanted to express through PINO the imperfection and weakness of robots, which have not been spotlighted so far.

Hiromura: I remember you consciously prepared many steps like taking a footprint of a baby when it is born, in order to make a story.


The outward design is the determinant of the image of everything


Kitano: In a sense, it suggests the direction of robot development. Robots are in close contact with users, their appearances are very important. The distance or closeness between a robot and its users is determined by its outside design. But this point has not been valued so much. If a robot moves on wheels, its function determines its style, and there is little that a designer can do to display his creativity. Or it is not interesting for a designer to design such a robot. For humanoids and products as Sony's AIBO, there are many things that designers can do. So, for PINO, I thought we should place priority on the design.

Hiromura: Do you mean that the exterior image played a great role in conveying the intention of the developer?

Kitano: It was the determinant. If we gave only a frame, then it would not have interested people, but its configuration meant a lot. It is a low-priced and low-tech robot. It cannot walk steadily like Honda's ASIMO. If PINO were 150 cm tall, it would be frightening to see it walking unsteadily. It is 70 cm tall, and we can accept it totters like a one-and-a-half-year old child. This height was the best considering parts.

Hiromura: Looking at PINO, I cannot help feeling how lovely it is. The image I get from its size and configuration may be geared unconsciously to the story of Pinocchio. It incites sympathy with something incomplete.

北野：しかも「ピノ」の場合は、通常の研究開発では考えにくいのですが、完全に完成していない段階で発表しているため、よけいに成長途中の子どものイメージが広がった。

デザインと工学のコラボレーション

北野：研究者というのは、どちらかといえばデザインの重要度を考えずにストレートに「じゃあ、人間の形にしてしまおう」とか考えてしまうのですが、その外観が実際にどういうメッセージを与えるのかを考える必要がある。それによって、我々がめざしているものを正しく表現できなければ、伝えたいことも伝わらなくなってしまうのですから。

廣村：僕は「ピノ」を最初に見た時、そのデザイン性の高さに衝撃を受けました。コミュニケーション能力が高いと思った。ロボットに限らず、これから科学、特に先端技術に携わる時には、表層となる意匠が非常に重要な意味を持ってくるなと感じた。

北野：特に、最終的に工業製品をめざすようなものでは重要になってきますね。産業とするために広くロボットに着手していくということになれば、技術だけではない。デザインと技術がマッチして、相互作用が起きた時にはじめて面白いものができる。デザインの力は実はすごく大きいんです。「ピノ」は、基礎研究という目的ももちろんありますが、それ以上に重要だったのはマーケティングとしての役割でした。現実の世の中で、ロボットというのがどのように扱われていくのか、そのポジショニングを「ピノ」によって探りたかった。工学というのは最終的には使われ、売られ、役に立ってこそのものです。社会におけるポジションがよく見えなければ方向性も定まらない。

廣村：デザインの側から見ても、これからのグラフィックやプロダクトの在り方は、そういう方向に行くように思います。技術ができあがった上で「はい、じゃあデザインをお願い」とオーダーされるのではなく、むしろそのコンテンツから考えていくような、根本から関わるべきなのがこれからのデザインだと思うのです。そうでなければデザイナーは単なる意匠屋でしかなくなってしまうのではないでしょうか。

北野宏明　サイエンティスト

1961年埼玉県生まれ。国際基督教大学教養学部理学科（物理学専攻）卒業後、日本電気（株）に入社、ソフトウエア生産技術研究所勤務。88年より米カーネギー・メロン大学客員研究員。91年京都大学博士号（工学）取得。93年ソニーコンピュータサイエンス研究所入社。96年同シニアリサーチャー、02年同取締役副所長就任。98年より科学技術振興事業団ERATO北野共生システムプロジェクト総括責任者兼務。ロボカップ国際委員会Founding President。国際ロボットデザイン委員会（IRoDA）理事。システム・バイオロジー研究機構会長。93年Computers and Thought Award、00年Prix Ars Electronica、97年JCDデザイン賞（日本商環境設計家協会）、01年日本文化デザイン賞受賞。ベネツィア・建築ビエンナーレ、ニューヨーク近代美術館（MoMA）等で招待展示を行う。著書に『システムバイオロジー』（秀潤社刊）、『大人のための徹底！ロボット学』（PHP研究所刊）等がある。

Kitano: In the case of PINO, we launched before it was perfected. This is unusual to do so in ordinary R&D projects. So, it may give an image of a boy in early childhood.

Collaboration between Designers and Engineers

Kitano: Researchers tend to conclude simply "OK, we will make it like a human figure" without considering the importance of design. It is necessary for them to think about what kind of images the outlook gives to people. Unless the end product can express what we are aiming at, we cannot convey our message to the public.

Hiromura: When I first saw PINO, I was surprised with its high quality design. I had an impression that it had the ability to communicate. Not only robots, but also products involving scientific technologies, especially, advanced technologies should have well-designed appearances.

Kitano: Particularly, if you are developing an industrial product, the importance of design increases. If we are going to create many more robots and develop a robotics industry, then we need interaction among people engaged in technology and design. In fact, the value of design is great. One of the aims of PINO was to promote basic research in robotics, of course. More important was its role in marketing. We wanted to survey how robots would be treated in society. PINO meant a probe for us. The goals of engineering are to study what will be used, sold, and help people to live a better life. So we cannot select which way we should take unless we know how a product in an R&D phase would be accepted by consumers.

Hiromura: Graphic and product designers should also take more interactive approaches with scientists and engineers. Instead of receiving orders for outside designs at the final stage of technological or engineering development, designers need to be involved from the very beginning of considering the contents. Otherwise, designers will be just subcontract illustrators.

Kitano Hiroaki, scientist

Born in Saitama in 1961. Upon graduation from the division of Natural Sciences (Physics), the School of Liberal Arts, International Christian University, employed by Software Engineering Laboratory, NEC Corporation. Visiting researcher at the Center for Machine Translation at Carnegie-Mellon University in the USA since 1988. Obtained Ph.D. in computer science from Kyoto University in 1991. Entered Sony Computer Science Laboratories, Inc. in 1993, became a senior researcher in 1996, and a Director in 2002. Since 1998, served also as a Project Director of ERATO Kitano Symbiotic Systems Project, Japan Science and Technology Corp. Founding President of The RoboCup Federation. Director of International Robot Design Associations, (IRoDA). President of the Systems Biology institute. Received the Computers and Thought Award from the International Joint Conferences on Artificial Intelligence in 1993, Commercial Space Design Award in 1997 (Japan Commercial Space Designers Association), Prix Ars Electronica in 2000, Japan Design Culture Award and Good Design Award in 2001. Invited artist for La Biennale di Venezia 2000, Worksphere exhibition at MoMA in 2001,etc. Published *Systems Biology* (Shujunsha), *Robotics for Adults* (PHP Research Institute).

設計データ

### 岩出山町立岩出山中学校

主要用途：中学校
所在地：宮城県玉造郡岩出山町
完成年月：1996年4月
敷地面積：201,811.00㎡
建築面積：6,757.17㎡
延床面積：10,879.06㎡
階数：地上3階、地下1階

### 埼玉県立大学

主要用途：大学
所在地：埼玉県越谷市
完成年月：1999年4月
敷地面積：102,265.37㎡
建築面積：34,030.77㎡
延床面積：54,080.11㎡
階数：地上4階

### 公立はこだて未来大学

主要用途：大学
所在地：北海道函館市
完成年月：2000年2月
敷地面積：166,403.77㎡
建築面積：13,287.03㎡
延床面積：26,839.55㎡
階数：地上5階

### ビッグハート出雲

主要用途：劇場を含む複合施設
所在地：島根県出雲市
完成年月：1999年12月
敷地面積：5,531.84㎡
建築面積：2,863.41㎡
延床面積：4,875.03㎡
階数：地上2階、地下1階

### 東証Arrows

主要用途：展示場、事務所
所在地：東京都中央区日本橋兜町
完成年月：2000年5月
敷地面積：7,192.99㎡
建築面積：5,220.67㎡
延床面積：49,627.82㎡
階数：地上16階、地下3階

### 名城大学

主要用途：大学
所在地：愛知県名古屋市
竣工予定：2002年12月
敷地面積：104,561.31㎡
建築面積：3,753.07㎡
延床面積：11,334㎡/共通講義棟（南）
延床面積：21,908㎡/高層棟
階数：地上5階/共通講義棟（南）
階数：地上16階、地下1階/高層棟

### 東京ウェルズテクニカルセンター

主要用途：研究所
所在地：静岡県沼津市
完成年月：2001年6月
敷地面積：1,945.49㎡
建築面積：639.19㎡
延床面積：1,279.99㎡
階数：地上3階

### CODAN Shinonome 1街区

主要用途：共同住宅、店舗
所在地：東京都江東区東雲
竣工予定：2003年4月
敷地面積：9,221.41㎡
建築面積：5,966.65㎡
延床面積：49,687.48㎡
階数：地上14階、地下1階

### 藤原新也 旅の軌跡展

展示内容：写真展
展示場所：駒ヶ根高原美術館
展示期間：2000年9月〜2001年2月
延床面積：1,600㎡
階数：2階

### 藤原新也 少年の港展

展示内容：写真展
展示場所：渋谷 パルコ
展示期間：1993年3月

### 藤原新也 アメリカ

展示内容：写真展
展示場所：渋谷 パルコ
展示期間：1990年11月

### 日本人とすまい 靴脱ぎ Kutsu-Nugi

主要用途：展示会
展示場所：リビングセンター OZONE
展示期間：1996年2月
展示スペース：700㎡

### 1999 竹尾ペーパーショウ

展示目的：販売促進
展示場所：青山スパイラルホール
展示期間：1999年4月
延床面積：836㎡
階数：地上3階

### 竹尾 見本帖本店

主要用途：販売促進スペース
所在地：東京都千代田区神田錦町
完成年月：2000年10月
敷地面積：527㎡
延床面積：762㎡
階数：2階

### 日本科学未来館

主要用途：科学館、研究施設
所在地：東京都江東区青海
完成年月：2001年7月
敷地面積：19,636.65㎡
建築面積：8,881.01㎡
延床面積：40,589.74㎡
階数：地上8階、地下2階、塔屋1階

### 札幌メディアパーク・スピカ

主要用途：他目的ホール
所在地：北海道札幌市
完成年月：2000年4月
敷地面積：8,472㎡
建築面積：3,865㎡
延床面積：13,446㎡
階数：地上2階、地下2階

### 横須賀市立美術館（仮称）

主要用途：美術館
所在地：神奈川県横須賀市
竣工予定：2007年
敷地面積：22,000㎡
建築面積：未定
延床面積：約6,500㎡
階数：未定

### 北野共生システムプロジェクト

主要用途：研究所
所在地：東京都渋谷区神宮前
完成年月：1999年3月
延床面積：640㎡（6階）、320㎡（7階）

# Plan Data

## Iwadeyama Junior High School

use : Junior High School
place : Iwadeyama Town,
Tamatsukuri-gun, Miyagi
completion : Apr. 1996
site area : 201,811.00㎡
building area : 6,757.17㎡
total floor area : 10,879.06㎡
number of stairs : 3 Floors, 1 Basement

## Saitama Prefectural University

use : University
place : Koshigaya City, Saitama
completion : Apr. 1999
site area : 102,265.37㎡
building area : 34,030.77㎡
total floor area : 54,080.11㎡
number of stairs : 4 Floors

## Future University-Hakodate

use : University
place : Hakodate City, Hokkaido
completion : Feb. 2000
site area : 166,403.77㎡
building area : 13,287.03㎡
total floor area : 26,839.55㎡
number of stairs : 5 Floors

## Big Heart Izumo

use : Cultural Complex Institution
place : Izumo City, Shimane
completion : Dec. 1999
site area : 5,531.84㎡
building area : 2,863.41㎡
total floor area : 4,875.03㎡
number of stairs : 2 Floors, 1 Basement

## Tokyo Stock Exchange Arrows

use : Exhibition Hall,Business Office
place : Kabuto-cho Nihombashi Chuo-ku Tokyo
completion : May. 2000
site area : 7,192.99㎡
building area : 5,220.67㎡
total floor area : 49,627.82㎡
number of stairs : 16 Floors, 3 Basements

## Meijo University

use : University
place : Nagoya City, Aichi
completion : Dec. 2002
site area : 104,561.31㎡
building area : 3,753.07㎡
total floor area : 11,334㎡ / Lecture Building
total floor area : 21,908㎡ / Tower
number of stairs : 5 Floors / Lecture Building
number of stairs : 16 Floors, 1 Basement / Tower

## Tokyo Weld Technical Center

use : Laboratory
place : Numazu City, Shizuoka
completion : Jun. 2001
site area : 1,945.49㎡
building area : 639.19㎡
total floor area : 1,279.99㎡
number of stairs : 3 Floors

## CODAN Shinonome District 1

use : Housing & Shop Complex
place : Shinonome, Koutou-ku, Tokyo
completion : Apr. 2003
site area : 9,221.41㎡
building area : 5,966.65㎡
total floor area : 49,687.48㎡
number of stairs : 14 Floors, 1 Basement

## Fujiwara Shinya "Travel Locus"

purpose : Photograph Exhibition
place : Komagane Kogen Art Museum
time : From Sep. 2000 To Feb. 2001
total floor area : 1,600㎡
number of stairs : 2 Floors

## Fujiwara Shinya "Syounen No Minato"

purpose : Photograph Exhibition
place : Shibuya Parco
time : Mar. 1993

## Fujiwara Shinya "America"

purpose : Photograph Exhibition
place : Shibuya Parco
time : Nov. 1990

## Japanese & Living Kutsu-Nugi

purpose : Exhibition
place : Living Center OZONE
time : Feb. 1996
space : 700㎡

## 1999 Takeo Paper Show

purpose : Sales Promotion
place : Aoyama Spiral Hall
time : Apr. 1999
total floor area : 863㎡
number of stairs : 3 Floors

## Takeo, Mihoncho Honten

use : Showroom of Shop
place : Kanda Nisiki-cho, Chiyoda-ku, Tokyo
competion : Oct. 2000
site area : 527㎡
total floor area : 732㎡
number of stairs : 2 Floors

## National Museum of Emerging Science and Innovation

211

use : Science Museum & Laboratory
place : Aomi, Koutou-ku, Tokyo
completion : Jul. 2001
site area : 19,636.65㎡
building area : 8,881.01㎡
total floor area : 40,589.74㎡
number of stairs : 8 Floors, 2 Basements, 1Tower

## Sapporo Media Park Spica

use : Multipurpose Hall
place : Sappro City, Hokkaido
completion : Apr. 2000
site area : 8,472㎡
building area : 3,865㎡
total floor area : 13,446㎡
number of stairs : 2 Floors, 2 Basements

## Yokosuka Museum of Art (provisional name)

use : Art Museum
place : Yokosuka City, Kanagawa
completion : 2007
site area : 22,000㎡
building area : Undecided
total floor area : 6,500㎡
number of stairs : Undecided

## Kitano Symbiotic Systems Project

use : Laboratory
place : Jingumae, Shibuya-ku, Tokyo
completion : Mar. 1999
total floor area : 640㎡(6F), 320㎡(7F)

1988 ・西友 岩見沢店 / CL：西友

1989 ・釧路フィッシャーマンズワーフ・MOO / CL：釧路河畔開発公社
　　　建築設計：毛綱毅曠

1990 ・海鮮 PAO（パオ）/ CL：東京 ROOF 実行委員会
　　　・藤原新也 アメリカ / CL：パルコ
　　　・KIDS PARK（キッズパーク）/ CL：西友

1991 ・赤羽 EPO（エポ）/ CL：西友
　　　・アロハシャツ展 / CL：リウボウ
　　　・木更津 EPO / CL：西友
　　　・西友 本八幡店 / CL：西友

1992 ・西友 田無店 / CL：西友
　　　・キッズファーム パオ / CL：西武百貨店
　　　・タラサ志摩 / CL：志摩東京カウンティ
　　　・石丸電気 Soft1（ソフトワン）/ CL：石丸電気
　　　建築設計：空建築設計ワーク
　　　・西友 岡崎店 / CL：西友

1993 ・藤原新也 少年の港展 / CL：パルコ
　　　・小田原 EPO（エポ）/ CL：西友
　　　・小倉玉屋 / CL：小倉玉屋
　　　・石丸電気 筑波店 / CL：石丸電気 / 建築設計：空建築設計ワーク
　　　・リゾートシティ ALTS 磐梯 / CL：磐梯リゾート開発

1994 ・亀老山展望公園 / CL：愛媛県越智郡吉海町 / 建築設計：隈研吾

1995 ・八代広域消防本部 / CL：八代広域行政組 / 建築設計：伊東豊雄
　　　・石丸電気 つくば2号店 テレビ館 / CL：石丸電気
　　　建築設計：空建築設計ワーク
　　　・日吉町ダム ビジターセンター / CL：水資源開発公団 / 建築設計：團紀彦
　　　・石丸電気 牛久店 / CL：石丸電気 / 建築設計：空建築設計ワーク

1996 ・日本人とすまい 靴脱ぎ / CL：オゾン / 展示設計：岡本好司
　　　・フードプラス藤枝店 / CL：西友
　　　・岩出山町立岩出山中学校 / CL：宮城県玉造郡岩出山町
　　　建築設計：山本理顕
　　　・ザ・モール安城 / CL：西友
　　　・近鉄百貨店 / CL：近鉄百貨店 / 内装設計：杉本貴志
　　　・西友 手稲店 / CL：西友
　　　・シープラザ釜石 / CL：岩手県釜石市
　　　・小田原市総合文化体育館小田原アリーナ / CL：神奈川県小田原市
　　　建築設計：坂倉建築設計事務所
　　　・フードプラス新座店 / CL：西友

1997 ・名古屋デザインミュージアム / CL：国際デザインセンター
　　　・横浜市下和泉地区センター、地域ケアプラザ / CL：神奈川県横浜市
　　　建築設計：山本理顕
　　　・横浜市東永谷地区センター、地域ケアプラザ / CL：神奈川県横浜市
　　　建築設計：伊東豊雄
　　　・石丸電気 水戸店 / CL：石丸電気 / 建築設計：空建築設計ワーク

212

1998 ・アムラックス サイン / CL：トヨタ自動車 / 内装設計：近藤康夫
　　　・大方 あかつき館 / CL：高知県大方町 / 建築設計：團紀彦
　　　・足摺テルメ / CL：高知県土佐清水市 / 建築設計：團紀彦
　　　・福島県民の森オートキャンプ / CL：福島県
　　　建築設計：トム ヘネガン
　　　・石丸電気 久喜店 / CL：石丸電気
　　　建築設計：空建築設計ワーク
　　　・ワールドジム サインデザイン / CL：ミトガワコーポレーション

1999 ・広島西消防署 / CL：広島県広島市 / 建築設計：山本理顕
　　　・石丸電気 柏店 / CL：石丸電気
　　　建築設計：空建築設計ワーク
　　　・津山グラスハウス / CL：岡山県津山市 / 建築設計：横河健
　　　・1999竹尾ペーパーショウ / CL：竹尾 / 会場構成：西沢立衛
　　　・ビッグハート出雲 / CL：島根県出雲市
　　　建築設計：小島一浩（シーラカンス アンド アソシエイツ）
　　　・埼玉県立大学 / CL：埼玉県立大学 / 建築設計：山本理顕
　　　・北野共生システムプロジェクト / CL：科学技術振興事業団
　　　内装設計：山本理顕

2000 ・LVMH / CL：インターアームリミテッド
　　　・札幌メディアパーク・スピカ / CL：札幌テレビ放送
　　　建築設計：伊坂重春
　　　・公立はこだて未来大学 / CL：公立はこだて未来大学
　　　建築設計：山本理顕
　　　・東証Arrows / CL：東京証券取引所 / 内装設計：近藤康夫
　　　・カッシーナ インターデコール ジャパン
　　　CL：カッシーナインターデコール ジャパン
　　　内装設計：近藤康夫
　　　・藤原新也 旅の軌跡展 / CL：駒ケ根高原美術館
　　　・Mタワー / CL：宮島商会 / 建築設計：團紀彦
　　　・アップグレード / CL：アップグレード / 内装設計：岡本好司
　　　・竹尾 見本帖本店 / CL：竹尾 / 内装設計：西沢立衛
　　　・丹沢湯彩 ほたる / CL：オリックスアルファ / 内装設計：新藤力
　　　・石丸電気 上尾店 / CL：石丸電気
　　　建築設計：空建築設計ワーク

2001 ・石丸電気 立川店 / CL：石丸電気
　　　建築設計：空建築設計ワーク
　　　・日本科学未来館 / CL：科学技術振興事業団
　　　建築設計：日建設計・久末設計設計共同企業体
　　　・東京ウェルズテクニカルセンター / CL：東京ウェルズ
　　　建築設計：山本理顕
　　　・道の駅 多古 / CL：千葉県多古町 / 建築設計：團紀彦
　　　・武蔵野市立 0123 はらっぱ / CL：東京都武蔵野市
　　　建築設計：横河健
　　　・タイガーシティ / CL：台湾 野美
　　　・ショッパーズ / CL：竹尾
　　　・BANビル / CL：吉田組 / 建築設計：山本理顕

2002 ・エスキス / CL：三菱商事 バブコック・アンド・ブラウン
　　　・泉ガーデン / CL：住友不動産 / 建築設計：日建設計
　　　・道の駅 栗源 / CL：千葉県栗源町 / 建築設計：團紀彦

1988 · SEIYU Iwamizawa Store / CL : The Seiyu

1989 · Kushiro Fisherman's Warf MOO
CL : Kushiro Water Front Development / ARCHI : Mozuna Kikou

1990 · KAISEN PAO / CL : Tokyo Roof Executive Committee
· Fujiwara Shinya "America" / CL : Parco
· KIDS PARK / CL : The Seiyu

1991 · Akabane EPO / CL : The Seiyu
· The Aloha Shirt Exhibition / CL : Ryobo
· Kisarazu EPO / CL : The Seiyu
· SEIYU Motoyawata Store / CL : The Seiyu

1992 · SEIYU Tanashi Store / CL : The Seiyu
· Kids Farm PAO / CL : The Seibu Department Stores
· Thalassa Shima / CL : Shima Tokyo County
· Ishimaru Denki Soft 1 / CL : Ishimaru Denki
ARCHI : Kuu Architect Work
· SEIYU Okazaki Store / CL : The Seiyu

1993 · Fujiwara Shinya "Syonen no Minato" / CL : Parco
· Odawara EPO / CL : The Seiyu
· Kokura Tamaya / CL : Kokura Tamaya
· Ishimaru Denki Tsukuba Store / CL : Ishimaru Denki
ARCHI : Kuu Architect Work
· Resort City ALTS Bandai / CL : Bandai Resort Development

1994 · Kirosan Panorama Park / CL : Yoshiumi Town, Ehime
ARCHI : Kuma Kengo

1995 · Yatsushiro Fire Station / CL : Yatsushiro Administration Union
ARCHI : Ito Toyo
· Ishimaru Denki Tsukuba Second Store TV Hall
CL : Ishimaru Denki / ARCHI : Kuu Architect Work
· Hiyoshi Town Dam Visitor Center
CL : Water Resources Development Corporation
ARCHI : Dan Norihiko
· Ishimaru Denki Ushiku Store / CL : Ishimaru Denki
ARCHI : Kuu Architect Work

1996 · Japanese and Living Kutsu-Nugi / CL : Ozone
exhibition plan : Okamoto Koji
· Food Plus Fujieda Store / CL : The Seiyu
· Iwadeyama Junior High School
CL : Iwadeyama Town, Miyagi / ARCHI : Yamamoto Riken
· The Mall Anju / CL : The Seiyu
· Kintetsu Department Store / CL : Kintetsu Department Store
INT.ARCHII : Sugimoto Takashi
· SEIYU Teine Store / CL : The Seiyu
· Sea-Plaza Kamaishi / CL : Kamaishi City, Iwate
· Odawara Arena / CL : Odawara City, Kanagawa
ARCHI : Sakakura Associates
· Food Plus Niiza Store / CL : The Seiyu

1997 · Nagoya Design Museum / CL : International Design Center Nagoya
· Shimoizumi Community Center, Care Plaza
CL : Yokohama City, Kanagawa / ARCHI : Yamamoto Riken
· Higashinagaya Community Center, Care Plaza
CL : Yokohama City, Kanagawa / ARCHI : Ito Toyo
· Ishimaru Denki Mito Store
CL : Ishimaru Denki / ARCHI : Kuu Architect Work

1998 · Amlux Sign / CL : Toyota Motor / INT.ARCHI : Kondoh Yasuo
· Ohgata Akatsuki-kan / CL : Ohgata Town, Kouchi / ARCHI : Dan Norihiko
· Ashizuri Therme / CL : Tosashimizu City, Kouchi / ARCHI : Dan Norihiko
· Automobile Camping Site. Fukushima People's Forest
CL : Fukushima Prefecture / ARCHI : Tom Henegan
· Ishimaru Denki Kuki Store / CL : Ishimaru Denki
ARCHI : Kuu Architect Work
· World Gym Sign Design / CL : Mitogawa Corporation

1999 · Hiroshima West Fire Service / CL : Hiroshima City, Hiroshima
ARCHI : Yamamoto Riken
· Ishimaru Denki Kashiwa Store / CL : Ishimaru Denki
ARCHI : Kuu Architect Work
· Tsuyama Glass House / CL : Tsuyama City, Okayama
ARCHI : Yokogawa Ken
· 1999 Takeo Paper Show / CL : Takeo / INT.ARCH : Nishizawa Ryue
· Big Heart Izumo / CL : Izumo City, Shimane
ARCHI : Kojima Kazuhiro(Coelacanth and Associates)
· Saitama Prefectural University
CL : Saitama Prefectural University / ARCHI : Yamamoto Riken
· Kitano Symbiotic Systems Project
CL : Japan Science and Technology
INT.ARCHI : Yamamoto Riken

213

2000 · LVMH / CL : Interarm LTD.
· Sappro Media Park Spica
CL : The Sapporo Television Broadcasting
ARCHI : Isaka Shigeharu
· Future University-Hakodate / CL : Future University-Hakodate
ARCHI : Yamamoto Riken
· Tokyo Stock Exchange Arrows
CL : Tokyo Stock Exchange / INT.ARCHI : Kondoh Yasuo
· Casina Inter-Décor Japan
CL : Casina Inter-Décor Japan / INT.ARCHI : Kondoh Yasuo
· Fujiwara Shinya "Travel Locus" / CL : Komagane Kogen Art Museum
· M Tower / CL : Miyajima Firm / ARCHI : Dan Norihiko
· Upgrade / CL : Upgrade / INT.ARCHI : Okamoto Koji
· Takeo, Mihoncho Honten / CL : Takeo / INT.ARCHI : Nishizawa Ryue
· Tanzawa Yusai Hotaru / CL : Orix Alpha
INT.ARCHI : Shindou Chikara
· Ishimaru Denki Ageo Store / CL : Ishimaru Denki
ARCHI : Kuu Architect Work

2001 · Ishimaru Denki Tachikawa Store / CL : Ishimaru Denki
ARCHI : Kuu Architect Work
· National Museum of Emerging Science and Innovation
CL : Japan Science and Technology
ARCHI : Nikken Kume Joint Trust
· Tokyo Weld Technical Center / CL : Tokyo Weld
ARCHI : Yamamoto Riken
· Michi no Eki Tako / CL : Tako Town, Chiba / ARCHI : Dan Norihiko
· 0123 Harappa Musashino Municipal / CL : Musashino City, Tokyo
ARCHI : Yokogawa Ken
· Tiger City / CL : Taiwan Nobi
· Shoppers / CL : Takeo
· Ban Building / CL : Yoshida Gumi / ARCHI : Yamamoto Riken

2002 · Esquisse / CL : Mitsubishi Corporation　Babcock & Brown
· Izumi Garden / CL : Sumitomo Realty & Development
ARCHI : Nikken Sekkei
· Michi no Eki Kurimoto / CL : Kurimoto Town, Chiba
ARCHI : Dan Norihiko

浅川敏
P66、67、68、69、72（下）、73（下）、76、77、78、79
東証Arrows
P184、185 札幌メディアパーク・スピカ

Asakawa Satoshi
P66, 67, 68, 69, 72(Lower), 73(Lower), 76, 77, 78, 79
Tokyo Stock Exchange Arrows
P184, 185 Sapporo Media Park Spica

大野繁
P108、109 CODAN Shinonome 1街区

Ohno Shigeru
P108, 109 CODAN Shinonome District 1

新建築社 写真部
P40、41 公立はこだて未来大学

Shinkenchiku-sha
P40, 41 Future University-Hakodate

高山幸三
P16、17、20、21、24、25、28、29、30、31 埼玉県立大学
P140、141、146、147 1999 竹尾ペーパーショウ
P152、153、154、155 竹尾見本帖本店
P194、195、197 北野共生システムプロジェクト

Takayama Kozo
P16, 17, 20, 21, 24, 25, 28, 29, 30, 31
Saitama Prefectural University
P140, 141, 146, 147 1999 Takeo Paper Show
P152, 153, 154, 155 Takeo, Mihoncho Honten
P194, 195, 197 Kitano Symbiotic Systems Project

中道淳（ナカサ＆パートナーズ）
P164、165、170、171 日本科学未来館

Nakamichi Jun(Nacasa&Partners)
P164, 165, 170, 171
National Museum of Emerging Science and Innovation

西沢立衛
P142、143（初期プランスケッチ）1999 竹尾ペーパーショウ

Nishizawa Ryue
P142, 143(First Plan Sketch) 1999 Takeo Paper Show

三島叡（日経BP社）
P26 埼玉県立大学

Mishima Satoru(Nikkei Business Publications)
P26 Saitama Prefectural University

平井広行
P52、53、57、60、64（上）、65（上、下中、下右）
ビッグハート出雲

Hirai Hiroyuki
P52, 53, 57, 60, 64(Upper), 65(Upper, Lower Center, Lower Right)
Big Heart Izumo

藤井保
P148、149、150、151 1999 竹尾ペーパーショウ 冊子

Fujii Tamotsu
P148, 149, 150, 151
1999 Takeo Paper Show booklet

藤塚光政
P8、9、10、11、13、14、15 岩出山町立岩出山中学校
P45、46、48 公立はこだて未来大学
P96、97、100、101、104、105
東京ウェルズテクニカルセンター
P182、183 札幌メディアパーク・スピカ

Fujitsuka Mitsumasa
P8, 9, 10, 11, 13, 14, 15 Iwadeyama Junior High School
P45, 46, 48 Future University-Hakodate
P96, 97, 100, 101, 104, 105 Tokyo Weld Techinical Center
P182, 183 Sapporo Media Park Spica

『ポケット版 東京二カ国語アトラス』梅田厚編 講談社インターナショナル
P47（上）

*The New Tokyo Bilingual Pocket Atlas* Umeda Atsushi Ed. / Kodansha International
P47 (Upper)

『標準 清人篆隷字彙』北川博邦編 雄山閣出版
P54、55、56

*Chinese Calligraphic Glossary* Kitagawa Hirokuni Ed. / Yuzankaku
P54, 55, 56

『銀河鉄道999』©松本零士・東映アニメーション
P168

*Galaxy Express 999* © Matsumoto Leiji / Toei Animation
P168

『KC DELUXE12 AKIRA PART2 アキラ』©大友克洋・講談社
P169（下右）

*KC DELUXE12 AKIRA PART2 AKIRA* © Otomo Katsuhiro / Kodansha
P169 (Lower Right)

『MeSci』日本科学未来館
P178、179、180、181

*MeSci* National Museum of Emerging Science And Innovation
P178, 179, 180, 181

廣村正彰 略歴

Hiromura Masaaki Profile

| | |
|---|---|
| 1954 | 愛知県生まれ |
| 1977 | 田中一光デザイン室 入社 |
| 1983 | 第17回SDA準部門賞 受賞 |
| 1987 | 日本グラフィックデザイナー協会 新人賞 受賞 |
| 1988 | 廣村デザイン事務所設立 |
| 1989 | 第23回SDA賞 受賞 |
| 1990 | 全国カタログポスター展 商工会議所会頭賞、<br>全国カレンダー展 部門賞、<br>第24回SDA奨励賞、DDA賞ディスプレイデザイン優秀賞、<br>JAA会長賞・生活文化部門 最優秀賞 受賞 |
| 1991 | ラハチポスタービエンナーレ佳作、<br>第25回準SDA賞・奨励賞 受賞 |
| 1992 | CSデザイン賞 銀賞、<br>日本タイポグラフィ協会 ベストワーク賞 受賞 |
| 1994 | 全国カタログポスター展 商工会議所会頭賞 受賞 |
| 1995 | 第62回毎日広告デザイン賞 部門賞、<br>N.Y.ADC 9th International Annual Exhibition 銀賞、<br>第29回SDA優秀賞、準優秀賞 受賞 |
| 1997 | 第65回毎日広告デザイン賞部門賞 受賞 |
| 1999 | 第33回SDA優秀賞 受賞 |
| 2000 | 第34回SDA準優秀賞 受賞 |
| 2001 | 2001年度グッドデザイン賞 受賞<br>第35回SDA優秀賞 受賞 |
| 2002 | CSデザイン賞金賞 受賞 |

| 1954 | Born in Aichi Prefecture, Japan. |
|---|---|
| 1977 | Joined Ikko Tanaka Design Studio. |
| 1983 | 17rd "Sign Design Category Award,"<br>Japan Sign Design Association (JSDA) |
| 1987 | "New Comers' Award," Japan Graphic Designers<br>Association JAGDA |
| 1988 | Established Hiromura Design Office Inc. Tokyo. |
| 1989 | 23rd "Sign Design First Prize," JSDA |
| 1990 | "Chairman's Award of the Chamber of Commerce<br>and Industry," Japan Catalog and Poster Exhibition<br>"National Calendar Exhibition Category Award"<br>24th "Sign Design Encouragement Prize," JSDA<br>"Display Design Second Award," Display Design Association<br>"Chairman's Award," Japan Advertising Association |
| 1991 | "Award of Merit" in Lahti XI Poster Biennial, Lahti Art Museum<br>25th " Sign Design Second Prize" and<br>"Encouragement Award," JSDA |
| 1992 | "Silver Award" in CS Design Award<br>"Best Work Award," Japan Typography Association |
| 1994 | "Chairman's Award of the Chamber of Commerce<br>and Industry," Japan Catalog and Poster Exhibition |
| 1995 | 62nd" Mainichi Design Category Award"<br>"Silver Award," N.Y. ADC 9th International Annual Exhibition<br>29th "Sign Design Second and Third Award," JSDA |
| 1997 | 65th "Mainichi Design Category Award" |
| 1999 | 33rd "Sign Design Second Award" JSDA |
| 2000 | 34th "Sign Design Third Award" JSDA |
| 2001 | "Good Design Award"<br>35th "Sign Design Second Award," JSDA |
| 2002 | 12th "CS Design Gold Award" |

215

スタッフ　小島利之、草谷隆文、金子正剛、小松原巧子、山本正子、
大高じゅん、相沢信彦、伊東幸子、以上元所員
水野佳史、木住野英彰、前田豊、別所恭子、望月一弘、
中尾千絵、塩津始子、以上現所員

STAFF　Kojima Toshiyuki, Kusagaya Takafumi, Kaneko Seigou,
Komatsubara Yoshiko, Yamamoto Masako, Ohtaka Jun,
Aizawa Nobuhiko, Itoh Sachiko (above, former employees)
Mizuno Yoshifumi, Kishino Hideaki, Maeda Yutaka,
Bessho Kyoko, Mochizuki Kazuhiro, Nakao Chie,
Shiozu Motoko (above, current employees)

SPACE GRAPHYSM

ISBN 90 6369 048 7

Published by BIS Publishers, Amsterdam

Copyright © 2003 BIS Publishers, Amsterdam

All rights reserved. No part of this publication may be reproduced or
transmitted in any form or by any means, electronic or mechanical, including
photocopy, recording or any information storage and retrieval system, without
permission in writing from the copyright owner(s).

Author: Hiromura Masaaki

Composing & Book Design: Hiromura Masaaki, Maeda Yutaka
Translation: Hayashi Chine
Writer for Interviews: Yoshihara Sayaka

First published In Japan, Rikuyosha Co., Ltd.
Shizuoka Bank Bldg.19-12 2-chome,
Shinjuku, Shinjuku-ku Tokyo Japan 160-0022
Tel: 81-3-3354-4020 Fax: 81-3-3352-3106
http://www.rikuyosha.co.jp/

© 2002 Hiromura Masaaki
© 2002 Rikuyosha Co., Ltd.
Printed in Japan by Toppan Printing Co., Ltd.